Anne Hébert

GW00702891

Les Fous de Bassan

Peter Noble

Reader in French
University of Reading

UNIVERSITY OF GLASGOW
FRENCH AND GERMAN PUBLICATIONS
1995

University of Glasgow French and German Publications

Series Editors: Mark G. Ward (German)
Geoff Woollen (French)

Consultant Editors: Colin Smethurst
Kenneth Varty

Modern Languages Building, University of Glasgow,
Glasgow G12 8QL, Scotland.

First published 1995.

Printed by Jasprint Ltd., Washington, Tyne & Wear.

ISBN 0 85261 470 5

Contents

Preface iv

Introduction 1

Chapter One **Structure** 5

Chapter Two **Symbolism** 9

Chapter Three **Sexuality** 16

Chapter Four **Non-narrators** 22

Chapter Five **Narrators** 29

Conclusion 59

Bibliography 65

Preface

The following study uses the text published by Éditions du Seuil (collection 'Points Roman', R141) in 1984. Page references are given in **bold type** between brackets. Details of other works and articles referred to are given in footnotes, or where possible incorporated into the text. Contributions by a critic who has written more than once on Hébert are designated by a name and keyword, e.g. Bishop, 'Énergie'; Slott, 'Submersion'.

I should like to express my warmest thanks to Walter Redfern and my wife, both of whom were kind enough to read the drafts of this book but bear no responsibility for the final version.

Reading, October 1995   Peter Noble

Introduction

Anne Hébert was born in 1916 at Sainte-Catherine de Fossambault (Québec province) into a family with a strong literary tradition. Her first cousin was the poet Saint-Denys Garneau, who was four years older than she was, and it was under his auspices that she published in 1942 her first collection of poems, *Les Songes en équilibre*. This was followed by *Le Tombeau des rois* (1953) and *Mystère de la parole*, which was added to *Le Tombeau* and published in 1960 as *Poèmes*. It was as a poet that Hébert first came to literary prominence, and she did not publish her first novel, *Les Chambres de bois*, until 1958, although there had been a collection of short stories, *Le Torrent*, in 1950. These two early prose works share the themes of her poetry: the difficulty of reconciling the real and the unreal, or the worlds of the body and the spirit, themes which recur in her later prose fiction.

Her first great success as a novelist was *Kamouraska*, which appeared in 1970, was subsequently translated into a dozen languages, and was made by Claude Jutia into a film (1973), the screenplay of which he wrote in collaboration with the author. Based on an event from Hébert's own family history, the novel describes the mental torment of Élisabeth Rolland as she waits for her second husband to die, an event which forces her to recall through flashbacks the murder of her first husband by her lover. This was followed by *Les Enfants du Sabbat* (1975), *Héloïse* (1980), *Les Fous de Bassan* (1982), *Le Premier Jardin* (1988), and *L'Enfant chargé de songes* (1992) and *Aurélien, Clara, Mademoiselle et le lieutenant anglais* (1995). Hébert is now recognised as a novelist of international stature and one of the leading novelists of French Canada, although in 1968 she moved to Paris and has lived there ever since.[1] All her novels are firmly rooted in her French-Canadian background and depend for much of their power on their setting. Her themes of the return to childhood, the importance of the mother, the movement between the real and the imaginary are all firmly anchored in the French-Canadian context, while retaining their universal appeal. Very much part of the poetic, literary tradition of Québec, Hébert is still an independent and striking figure whose novels do not easily fit into any category. Québec supplies the basic material of plot and setting, which she then uses for her own purposes.

---

[1] Hébert's decision to live in France has been bitterly by criticised by certain Québec critics, criticisms which have clearly hurt their victim. See *Anne Hébert, son œuvre, leurs exils* (Presses Universitaires de Bordeaux, 1993), pp. 94-8, for some striking examples, well analysed by author Neil B. Bishop.

Les Fous de Bassan is the fifth novel and is thought by many critics to show the author at her best.[2] As Kathryn Slott's recent article[3] makes clear, the film adaptation by Yves Simoneau (1987) changes the emphasis somewhat, as can also be anticipated from the lurid cinema poster that is currently reproduced on the cover of the reference edition. It is not proposed to analyse the film here, but rather to concentrate on a many-layered piece of prose fiction, rich in symbolism, with a complicated structure moving between 1982 (for the two narrators who open and close the book) and the summer of 1936 (when the events which inspired the novel took place). The other voices which relate fragments of the story are either undated (but clearly from someone no longer alive), as in the case of Olivia de la Haute Mer, or contemporaneous with the events which they describe, although they include flashbacks to even earlier events from the childhood of the different narrators, a technique which Anne Hébert increasingly uses in her novels (Gasquy-Resch, pp. 134-5). The narrative set in 1982 is divided between Nicolas Jones, the pastor of the community of Griffin Creek, and his nephew Stevens Brown, who writes to his friend Michael Hotchkiss in Florida both in 1936 and 1982. Stevens's cousin Nora Atkins, the ghost of another cousin, Olivia Atkins, Stevens's brother Perceval who is a simpleton and *autres voix* share the narrative of 1936 with Stevens.[4] All the narrators are related, as Nicolas Jones is the uncle of the four younger narrators. All are concerned with events which lead up to the murder of Nora and Olivia, and the aftermath of the murder which eventually brings about the disintegration of what had been a flourishing, if isolated, community.

Griffin Creek, which the author stresses in her 'Avis au lecteur' is a purely imaginary 'Espace romanesque où se déroule une histoire sans aucun rapport avec aucun fait réel ayant pu survenir entre Québec et l'océan Atlantique' (**9**), lies on the shore of the St. Lawrence and was settled by English-speaking loyalists in flight from the rebellious American colonies. There were four main families, the Joneses, the Browns, the Atkinses and the Macdonalds, all of which survived into the 1930s, intermarrying and breeding

---

[2] Though not Suzanne Lamy, 'Le Roman de l'irresponsabilité', *Spirale*, 29 (novembre 1982), 3; 2, who takes *Les Fous de Bassan* to task for its banal romanticism and reworking of over-familiar Hébertian themes.

[3] 'From Agent of Destruction to Object of Desire: The Cinematic Transformation of Stevens Brown in *Les Fous de Bassan*', *Québec Studies*, 9 (1989-1990), 17-28.

[4] Marilyn Randall, 'Les Énigmes des *Fous de Bassan:* féminisme, narration et clôture', *Voix et Images*, 43 (automne 1989), 76-7, states interestingly that the whole work could be seen as the work of Stevens, certainly the only one who actually writes: the other narrations are all internal monologues. Conferring on Stevens the responsibility for the text would undermine a feminist interpretation of the book, and Randall points out that the film used this technique, in this way depriving the girls of their own voices. Although the rest of Randall's critique of a feminist interpretation remains valid, her view of Stevens is problematised by Hébert's own rejection of it.

prolifically, but isolated by their language and their religion from their neighbours. They are poor farmers and fisherman who are also keen hunters, and the society is a very traditional, patriarchal one in which the men and women lead largely separate lives and where the same standards are not expected of men and women. Hébert deliberately chose this setting to heighten the sense of strangeness and isolation, to convey what she had felt on reading English novels in translation.[5] She does not, however, put this isolated English community at odds with the surrounding French majority.[6] The community is totally self-contained, and there are only two clues given to the fact that it has not been absorbed by the French. All the Christian names are English, Sidney, Nora, etc, and the detective McKenna who investigates the murder has been chosen for the case because he speaks English: 'Il est de langue anglaise et plus habile à confesser les gens qu'un prêtre catholique'(189).

Isolated, self-contained, inbred and introverted, the community contains the seeds of its own destruction. The characters come to realise that they are responsible for the disaster which overtakes the village, and that the community as a whole cannot avoid a share of the guilt. The pastor can see that evil had entered the soul of the village long before the events which are actually described and that tragedy in some form was the probable result. His grim and gloomy faith reflects the influence of Jansenism, which is to be found elsewhere in the work of Hébert and permeates this novel with its acceptance of the inevitability of fate and of the sinful nature of man.[7]

In this way the story is far more than a murder story whose narrative builds up to revealing the identity of the killer. It attempts to examine the forces which bring about the murder, to study the tensions and strains within the community, and takes a deeply pessimistic view of the relations between men and women. By the end of the book nothing is left of the community except a handful of elderly survivors, led by the pastor, all waiting to die in Griffin Creek, and Stevens, a veteran of the Second World War and permanent invalid suffering from mental delusions, who is marooned

[5] 'Ce roman, je ne voulais pas l'écrire en anglais, mais je voulais donner l'impression que j'ai ressentie souvent en lisant des romans anglais en français. Je voulais donc qu'il y ait une sorte de dépaysement; alors j'ai voulu filtrer les mots anglais sans pour autant faire couleur locale; les mots anglais sont là pour faire résonner l'étrangeté de vie là-bas'—Hébert, in an interview with Brigitte Morissette, 'Lointaine et proche Anne Hébert', *Châtelaine* (février 1983), pp. 53-4.

[6] Ronald Ewing, 'Griffin Creek. The English World of Anne Hébert', *Canadian Literature*, 105 (Summer 1985), 105: 'There is no recognition of the French fact by the people of Griffin Creek. [...]. Since their ancestors were the first to settle in the area and did not mix with outsiders, they are not likely to feel guilty or be guilty for the political situation in Quebec.'

[7] Antoine Sirois, 'Bible, Mythes et *Fous de Bassan*', *Canadian Literature*, 104 (Spring 1985), 180: 'Tout est parallèle mais aussi analogie entre les actions de Griffin Creek et celles du Jardin d'Éden... À la faute succédera la punition...'

in Montréal writing letters which he may never post to his friend in
Florida who may be dead, letters in which he will finally reveal the
truth as he sees it about the summer of 1936. Even after Stevens's
admission to old Mic that he was the murderer of his cousins there
remains an ambiguity. Can the word of a war-crazed invalid living
on pills which he has stolen from the pharmacy be trusted, or is his
delusion simply obscuring the guilt of someone else who is
unprepared to admit the truth? After all, Nicolas, his uncle, was on
the beach that night.

Chapter One

Structure

The narrative is divided into six unequal sections, of which three are described as *livres:* 'le livre du révérend Nicolas Jones', 'le livre de Nora Atkins', 'le livre de Perceval Brown et de quelques autres'. The Biblical echo in the word *livre* is surely deliberate, and the mixture of masculine and feminine narrators is perhaps reminiscent of the Old Testament.[1] Both the contributions of Stevens are 'lettres', 'lettres de Stevens Brown à Michael Hotchkiss' and 'dernière lettre de Stevens Brown à Michael Hotchkiss', while the section attributed to Olivia de la Haute Mer is not defined. The different titles convey the different intentions of the narrators. Olivia, the spirit, returning to haunt the shores of her childhood is communing with herself as she laments over what happened.[2] The letters of Stevens enable him to explain to himself what is happening and has happened, as he endeavours to set things out logically for old Mic; even after the passing of forty-six years with no contact between the two correspondents, he feels able to confide more easily in him than in any other human being, certainly any of his relations. The book of Nicolas Jones serves to introduce the tragedy, to create the atmosphere of the village and, by showing at the beginning of the narrative what the outcome has been for the village, prepares the reader for the tragedy of the summer of 1936. Past and present are inextricably entwined in Nicolas's mind, as neither he nor his twin servants Pam and Pat, the sisters of Stevens and Perceval, can forget that long-distant summer. Unlike Stevens, however, he is not prepared to face the dreadful nature of the events or his own role in their unfolding, so that his book truly serves as an introduction hinting at what is to come but shying away from the truth.

The book of Nora is set in 1936, and contains flashbacks to her childhood which foreshadow the events of a year when Nora realised that she had left childhood behind her and could look forward to womanhood with joyful anticipation. The book of Perceval which also contains flashbacks takes the narrative forward, as Nora cannot include what happens after she and Olivia left the house of Maureen Macdonald, the last time they were seen alive, except by their murderer. Perceval is a witness to the interrogation of Stevens by the

---

[1] Sirois, p. 178, finds over a hundred references to the Bible, especially *Genesis* and *Exodus*.

[2] Bishop, 'Distance, point de vue, voix et idéologie dans *Les Fous de Bassan* d'Anne Hébert', *Voix et Image,* 9 (1984), part 2, p. 115: 'le livre d'Olivia de la Haute Mer fait alterner le récit du passé (enfance d'Olivia, été 1936, soir du 31 août 1936) et celui de sa "vie" présente'.

police, and to many other things which he will not admit to having seen. Other voices contribute to his narrative to describe scenes which he could not have witnessed, so that gradually the reader can build up a picture of what was happening during the search for the missing girls and the following police investigation, much in the way that the inhabitants of Griffin Creek must have done at the time.

> Nous les gens de Griffin Creek, devancés par les événements, ne pouvant plus suivre, bouleversés par la disparition de Nora et d'Olivia, n'ayant pas le temps de faire entre nous les recoupements nécessaires, mis en face de la police et sommés de répondre, sans avoir le temps de se consulter et de réfléchir. (**157**)

The community as a whole reacts to the disappearances by playing for time and trying to maintain a common front when faced with the police. In fact it closes ranks to protect Stevens, afraid of the dishonour for the community. Perceval could not convincingly utter such thoughts so elegantly formulated, but they are an essential part of the narrative. In this way, fragments of the story are put together to make an incomplete picture, and the missing bits are supplied only forty-six years later when Stevens writes his final letter.

Fragmentation of time and narrator is a technique which Anne Hébert has used before, in *Kamouraska* for example, where the narrative is constantly switching between the different periods of the life of Élisabeth and also between the different personalities which she assumed, Élisabeth d'Aulnières, Madame Tassy and Madame Rolland, each of whom narrates part of the story. Occasionally the omniscient narrator also intervenes. In *Les Fous de Bassan,* the technique is taken further, and the interventions of the external narrator are reduced to a minimum. One of the rare examples occurs in the narrative of Nicolas Jones:

> Le soir du barn dance Nicolas Jones danse avec les petites Atkins, les fait tourner et virevolter à tour de rôle, les tient par la main et par la taille, respire leur odeur à plein nez. (**46**)[3]

Nicolas Jones is also a many-faceted personality, because he is not only the man of God, who has known his destiny since he was a teenager. To his shame he has a darker side to his nature, which makes him close to the other men of Griffin Creek. The episode in which he spies like a voyeur on his mother and her granddaughters, his nieces, as they bathe in the sea at dawn, is narrated in the third person by the pastor, as he seeks to distance himself from his narrative and the events described in it. Aware of his unadmitted

---

[3] Bishop, 'Distance', p. 116. See also the intrusion into Perceval's book quoted below, p. 32.

desires, the pastor does not wish to identify himself too closely with his younger self lusting incestuously after his own kin. The use of the third person allows Hébert to express both the longing and the disgust in the pastor's mind without intervening herself directly. The pastor's feelings are further underlined by the presence of his teenage nephew, Perceval, who is present on the the the beach for the same purpose as the pastor, although Perceval's desires are neither so shameful nor so unadmitted as those of the pastor.

By the use of different voices all the main characters in the drama are able to contribute to the narrative. The reader can in this way participate in the emotions of each narrator, and Hébert can give different views of the events. They are seen through the eyes of the guilt-ridden pastor looking back over forty-six years; narrated by Stevens in his letters from the time of his return to the village on 20 June up to the last few minutes before the disappearance of the girls and their murder; by Nora from 14 July up to the time when she and Olivia leave the house of Maureen Macdonald; by Perceval and others from the evening of the murder to the moment when the policeman, McKenna, arrests Stevens; by the ghost of Olivia returning at some unknown point between 1936 and 1982, not for the first or the last time, to haunt the beach where she died and revisit the house where she had lived; finally by Stevens, now unbalanced, in his last letter to his friend in which he tries to come to terms with the past and to give his version of what happened.

The difference of voices is crucial to the development of the narrative as Hébert aims to provide the reader with the pieces of the puzzle in the way that the participants themselves might have gradually pieced them together.[4] Authorial licence is exercised in allowing the return of the spirit of Olivia to add her contribution, but even this is not wholly fantastic. Many feel themselves to be in touch with the spirit world by a variety of means, even today. The care which Hébert takes to differentiate between the different styles of the narrators, the adolescent temperament of Nora, the gloom and selfishness of the eighty-year-old pastor, for example, renders improbable the theory that all the voices are different manifestations of Stevens's voice, his inner demons tormenting him.[5]

---

[4] Bishop, 'Distance', p. 117: 'l'un des buts que vise cette écriture est la création et le maintien du suspense'.

[5] Jean-Louis Backès, 'Le Retour des morts dans l'œuvre d'Anne Hébert', *L'Esprit créateur*, XXIII, 3 (Fall 1983), 56: 'ce lecteur négligera tranquillement, dans sa grande soif de vérité, les phrases où il est dit et que Stevens est malade, et que la justice a considéré ses aveux comme extorqués.' This seems to ignore the clear indications in Olivia's account that Stevens is the murderer whom she is seeking, although admittedly she never names him. See also Randall, p. 66: 'Et l'incertitude se concrétise jusqu'à s'inscrire dans la phrase finale du texte, où Stevens admet que ses aveux ont été *rejetés par la cour et considérés comme extorqués et non conformes à la loi*.' Again, the book's final words do not mean that his confession was necessarily false. Hébert is making it clear to the reader why Stevens did not spend the rest of his life in prison,

Not only is time fragmented, but so also is syntax. Hébert is fond of using broken or incomplete sentences, and the way that she manipulates silences can add to the meaning of what has just been said.

> —Dis-le, dis-le qu'elle est jolie!
> Mon père fronce les sourcils. Il craint que je ne devienne vaniteuse.
> Préfère se taire. Quitte la pièce sans me regarder. (**134**)

The reluctance of Nora's father to flatter her, sensing perhaps the risks that lie ahead for such a pretty girl, and his embarrassment at being put on the spot by his wife are brought out by both the picture of him frowning and his hasty exit, emphasised by the absence of subject pronouns in the last two sentences. Her narrative closes with the words 'Fin de l'été' (**135**), as she looks forward to the new school year, her last, contrasting her life with that of her older cousin Olivia, who has three men to look after. The finality of the words anticipates the end of her life, which will follow in a few minutes. The irony of her optimistic anticipation of the new school year is brought out by these words, which suggest an end, not a new beginning as she intends. They prepare the way for the next section, in which Perceval and others will describe the night after the girls have failed to return home and in which it gradually becomes clear that they have disappeared. Syntax becomes a tool of narrative and an essential part of the structure, just as it was in *Kamouraska*.

Chapter Two

Symbolism

The use of symbols by Anne Hébert adds greatly to the richness of the narrative. The very date, 1936, is rich in numerical symbolism. *One* is the number of God, and *three* the number of the Trinity as well as the virtues. Three keeps recurring in the book as in the three days and nights of the storm. *Nine* is the number of the end and the beginning, while *six* is the number of sin which marks the Antichrist in the Apocalypse. Stevens is sixty-six when he writes his last letter to old Mic, and his is the sixth book of the novel, so that his symbolic link with evil is clear. Stevens's other book is the second, and *two* is the number of deceit and ambivalence. In it he is preparing the way for the sixth book, which clearly reveals his surrender to evil. In his sixth book he is announcing the end of the world which they all knew, the end of Griffin Creek. By way of contrast, Nora's book is the third, and *three* is the number of perfection. Hers is the book of life before the Fall, in which she sees herself as an 'Ève nouvelle'. *Four* is the number of the cross, of the four evangelists and in the fourth book Perceval is often prophetic and apocalyptic foreseeing the end of the world and the transformation of his dead cousins so that they become at one with nature. The fifth book is Olivia's, and on the fifth day of the creation God created the beasts of the sea and the air. Olivia as a disembodied spirit born on the wind and seeking shelter in the waves belongs to both elements, drawn back to Griffin Creek on 31 August, the exact reversal of her birthday, 13 June. *Thirteen* is the symbol of a perpetual rebeginning, but not a rebirth, which describes exactly the state of limbo in which the unburied ghost finds herself. The same link with *Genesis* can be found in the first book of Nicolas Jones which quotes from its opening verses at the beginning and again at the end in a way which symbolises their emptiness. In this way, the six books of *Les Fous de Bassan* correspond to the six days of Creation (on the seventh, God rested), and Christian symbolism can be seen to be central to the construction of the book (Mésavage, pp. 113-23).

The other symbols are mostly drawn from nature and belong to the harsh, inhospitable setting of the St. Lawrence Gulf, where the village, Griffin Creek, lies between two headlands, Cap Sec and Cap Sauvagine. Griffin suggests the mythical bird, the griffon with its double symbolism of the lion and the eagle, Christ and the devil.[1]

---

[1] Mésavage, p. 111. See also Annabelle Rea, 'The Climate of Viol/Violence and Madness in Anne Hébert's *Les Fous de Bassan*', *Quebec Studies*, 4 (1986), 172.

The names of the capes evoke the remoteness and the harshness of the region. The setting is arid and wild, unwelcoming to the refugees from the south who had to settle there and carve out a new life for themselves. The roughness and difficulty of the the land will be reflected in the people, who are themselves violent, passionate and unforgiving. They feel that the land is truly theirs, as they did not displace either French or Indians when they settled it and proceeded to make it habitable. For them it was a sort of promised land, which God had reserved for them when they fled from the rebellious colonies. They see themselves as a chosen people. All around them are the sea and the wind, which almost never stops blowing. Both the pastor and his nephew, Stevens, attribute much of the blame for the events of 1936 to the wind which permeates every moment of the lives of the inhabitants of Griffin Creek. The sea provides a living for the men, but a harsh and dangerous one. More importantly, it symbolises the ideas of change and continuity which are associated with the female characters in the book: change because the sea is never the same, and continuity because it is everlasting.

The local wildlife is represented in particular by 'les fous de Bassan';[2] these are gannets in English, a word which lacks the polysemous potential of standard French, the only extra Anglo-Saxon meaning available being the idiomatic 'greedy person'. The title of the English translation, *In the Shadow of the Wind,* points to one of the major themes in the book—the all-pervading wind—but fails to convey the symbolism of the French original. Gannets are large, white, noisy seabirds which nest in huge colonies in remote areas and hunt their food by diving spectacularly into the sea to catch it. Aggressive and quarrelsome when they are together, they disperse to sea in winter.[3] Their name, *fous,* refers to their relative lack of fear of men, which made them a possible prey, but here the title refers not just to the local gannets. Closely linked to the symbolism of the birds are the ideas associated with them of noise, height and depth. Their colours, black and white, are found repeatedly in the narrative as is the colour red. Irène Jones sees in the hair pigmentation of Nora and Nicolas a visible reminder of the closeness of the relationship between them.

> —Tout le monde sait que les deux plus roux de Griffin Creek se ressemblent, comme père et fille: bien qu'ils ne soient que l'oncle et la nièce. (45)

---

[2] See, among other references, **39; 42; 166; 238.**

[3] Ewing, p. 109, draws other parallels between inhabitant and bird. 'The symbol of the gannets is twofold. Once Griffin Creek seemed as prolific as a gannet colony; now it most resembles the deserted nests of the gannets. Such is the final image of Hébert's English world.'

Black is particularly associated with the pastor. It is a colour of death, mourning and guilt, expressing the depressed and depressing outlook of the man, who is haunted by events which he is unwilling to face up to. Touches of white remind the reader that he is the local minister of religion, but the black in which he is dressed is the colour linked to men and their violence. White is associated particularly with the moon, which is also a symbol of evil and mystery.[4] It is, of course, by moonlight that the crime takes place, and Stevens comments that Perceval's mental stability is always affected by the moon: he is truly lunatic. On the last night Stevens himself is bathed in moonlight and his appearance strangely altered. The blackness of the night and the whiteness of the moon combine to create a sinister atmosphere, appropriate to the thoughts and deeds of Stevens and the other characters. Other colours, red, violet, orange, are associated with the women. Maureen's garden is full of colour from the many flowers she grows there. Red can be the symbol of grief (Hillenaar, p. 14), of desire (Roy, p. 153), or the fires of Hell and of treason, since Judas Iscariot is traditionally represented as red-haired like the pastor (Francoli, p. 133). Nora revels in the redness of her hair and contrasts it with the blondness of Olivia, unaware of its possible symbolism. The women claim for themselves the dawn and the sunrise, when the sky is flushed with pink, an almost sacred hour reserved for its female devotees, in which Felicity initiates her granddaughters into the peace and beauty of a time without men.

A leitmotif of the book is the memory of the ancestors and, for Olivia in particular, the warnings of their voices which are carried on the wind. The wind is everywhere in the novel, and all the characters are aware of its influence. The pastor has no doubt about the importance of the wind.

> Dans toute cette histoire il faudrait tenir compte du vent, de la présence du vent, de sa voix lancinante dans nos oreilles, de son haleine salée sur nos lèvres. Pas un geste d'homme ou de femme, dans ce pays, qui ne soit accompagné par le vent [...]. Le vent a toujours soufflé trop fort ici et ce qui est arrivé n'a été possible qu'à cause du vent qui entête et rend fou. (26)

From the earliest pages the wind is linked to the madness of the characters, few of whom escape. Stevens chimes in with his uncle in identifying this element: 'Dans toute cette histoire, je l'ai déjà dit, il faut tenir compte du vent. Du commencement à la fin' (246). The

---

[4] Bishop, 'Énergie textuelle et production de sens: images de l'énergie dans *Les Fous de Bassan* d'Anne Hébert', *University of Toronto Quarterly*, 2 (hiver 1984-1985), 187: 'Olivia, évoquant la funeste soirée aoûtienne, revoit Stevens sous cette lumière lunaire que lui-même a qualifiée de maléfique.'

fury of the wind matches the torment which rages inside his head once he is back in Griffin Creek. The three-day tempest, with its noise and unchained energy, fills Stevens with such excitement that his Uncle Ben, the father of Nora, thinks that he is drunk when he totters into their house. Nora, however, shrewdly realises that it is not alcohol which is making Stevens possessed but the excitement within him which is responding to the wildness of the elements (**133**). Stevens is so involved with the wind that he is convinced that the wind was blowing a gale during the period of the crime, even though everyone else is well aware that the evening was a flat calm, with a beautiful, cold moon.

> Tout le monde dans la région est d'accord pour assurer qu'il n'y avait pas de vent ce soir-là et que la mer n'avait jamais été aussi paisible. Et pourtant, moi, Stevens Brown, fils de John Brown et de Bea Brown, j'affirme que subitement quelque chose s'est rompu dans l'air tranquille, autour de nous. La bulle fragile dans laquelle nous étions encore à l'abri crève soudain et nous voilà précipités, tous les trois, dans la fureur du monde. (**243-4**)

His inner torment is symbolised by the weather, which he alone seems to experience. With Nora dead, there is a brief lull.

> Un petit silence. Un tout petit silence pour reprendre haleine. La paix du monde autour de nous un instant encore. (**245**)

Then he turns to Olivia, who is already seeking refuge in flight, and catches her by the ankles. As the worst violence in the novel takes place, Stevens swears that the wind rages again.

> Tous vont insister sur le calme de la nuit, l'absence de vent. Et moi j'affirme avoir éprouvé la rage de la tempête dans tout mon corps secoué et disloqué, tandis qu'Olivia se débattait, partageant avec moi le même ressac forcené. (**246**)

For Stevens, the wind is not only the symbol of his fury, it is the partner in his crime, which raises the skirts of Olivia, opening the way for his rape (Bishop, 'Énergie textuelle', p. 188). The noise of the wind covers the cries of Olivia, and Stevens in his turn shouts frenziedly, trusting in the wind to drown the noise.

For the men the wind is responsible for the evil, the symbol and the partner in the crime, but for the women it can have another meaning. Olivia knows that with the wind come the voices of her female ancestors, warning her against Stevens. Normally she is protected by her father and her brothers who rarely leave her unsupervised, but whenever Stevens appears she hears the voices of her dead mother and grandmothers:

> Et le vent qui tourbillonne tout autour de la maison fait résonner Griffin Creek avec des voix de femmes patientes, repasseuses, laveuses, cuisinières, épouses, grossissantes, enfantantes, mères des vivants et des morts, désirantes et désirées dans le vent amer. [...] une cohorte de femmes dans l'ombre et le vent la priant de continuer à repasser comme si de rien n'était. **(215)**

They can sense the evil in Stevens. When he suddenly appears while Olivia is hanging out the washing, the voices of her ancestors return **(216)**. Her dead mother, whom she adored, whispers to her that Stevens cannot be trusted:

> Ma mère, parmi elles, la plus fraîche et la plus salée à la fois, me parle en secret ma douce langue natale et me dit de me méfier de Stevens. **(217)**

If the wind is important for Olivia, bringing her warnings from the dead, it is the sea that is important for Nora, not because it warns her but because she feels part of it, and it is from it that she came:

> Ce n'est pas pour rien que je joue si souvent au bord de la mer. J'y suis née. C'est comme si je me cherchais moi-même dans le sable et l'eau. **(116)**

She feels that in another life she was a sea creature, able to survive in the sea without breathing. As a swimmer, she never has the same mastery of the sea as Olivia, trained by her brother Patrick, but still in her dreams she recalls her former power over it. For Nora, Olivia and their grandmother Felicity, the sea represents freedom. Freedom from the men who dominate their lives. Freedom from the everyday chores of running a house and looking after a family, with which only Nora, at fifteen the youngest of the trio, is not yet saddled. At dawn, Felicity takes her granddaughters to the sea where they bathe in the freezing waters of the Atlantic, an occasion from which men are excluded. For an hour or so the women are their own mistresses, and the sea symbolises their freedom. It is also their refuge, where Olivia floats forever as a disembodied spirit brought in by the tide, washed out by the tide, always returning to haunt Griffin Creek, to which she is drawn by her unsatisfied desire. The sea is the one area where the women can escape from the men (Senécal, p. 151). The men do not share their fascination with the sea, and cannot follow the women in their return to the womb from which all human life ultimately sprang.[5] The pastor and Perceval

---

[5] Kathryn Slott, 'Repression, Obsession and Re-emergence in Hébert's *Les Fous de Bassan*,' *American Review of Canadian Studies*, XVII, 3 (1987), 303: 'Nicolas, Stevens and Perceval, all jealous of the exclusive attention of Felicity, try to molest Nora and Olivia on the shore, but never in the water.'

resent their exclusion from this group, but they fear the authority of
Felicity too much to intrude.

The sea is also the domain of the birds which give the book its
title. It provides them with food which they capture by diving into it
with great force from a considerable height, their long, sharp beaks
thrusting the water aside in pursuit of their prey. The sexual
symbolism of this cannot be ignored, especially when the sea is so
obviously associated with women and represents the womb from
which everything sprang. The birds, which are linked by their name
to the people of the locality—the words *fou* or *folie* appear on
almost every page to describe one or other of the characters[6]—,
violate the sea in their need to survive and preserve their species, as
the men of the region violate their women either in or outside
marriage. The noise of the birds is linked to the noise of the wind.
Stevens is sure that the birds were as noisy as the wind on the night
of the murders, although everyone else is sure that they were utterly
quiet. Stevens swears that great, screeching bands of seabirds
wheeled over the beach where he lay with Nora and Olivia, and
forty-six years later he can still hear their noise. The sound of their
wings fills his room in Montréal:

> Feindre d'ignorer les battements d'ailes claquant dans toute la chambre.
> Toiture et plafond à présent ouverts et défoncés à coups de becs durs.
> **(237)**

Yet he admires these birds, which he describes as 'superbe[s]' **(238)**,
and which he has spent hours watching. They are part of the natural
forces which represent the unchained energy which is in Stevens, and
which he uses so destructively against the people of Griffin Creek.
Not all birds share the somewhat sinister symbolism of the gannets,
however. The thrushes and blackbirds which peer in at Nora's
window at dawn, when she rises to go swimming with her
grandmother, represent her alert and curious state of mind. Nora is
even more closely linked with nature when she is about to carry
refreshments into the forest to the hunters. Her mother warns her to
take great care, because with her red hair she could easily be
mistaken for a deer and killed by the very men she is trying to feed.
The threat posed by men to women is clearly symbolised in the
animal imagery, and is underlined when Nora actually reaches the
hunters. The reactions of her cousin Sidney and her uncle, the

---

[6] Janet Paterson, 'L'Envolée de l'écriture: *Les Fous de Bassan* d'Anne Hébert', *Voix et Images*,
IX, 3 (printemps 1984), 144, discusses the significance of the title as an indicator of *folie*. On the
following page she analyses the sexual symbolism of the references to the birds in the book of
Nicolas Jones.

pastor, alarm her father, who rapidly orders her back to the house, away from the implied threat posed by her male relations.

Another important symbol is the role played by the spirits of the other world. Olivia in her own narrative is a *revenant,* brought back to Griffin Creek by the power of the sea and the wind to which she has returned, but also by the power of her desire which was unsatisfied while she was on earth. Her return and her unearthly presence can be seen as symbols of the feminine need both for physical satisfaction and also for peace. It must surely be significant that it is the unburied Olivia who returns to haunt the scene of the crime. Nora, whose corpse was washed up by the tide, is buried in the churchyard, and her spirit seems to be at peace. Olivia is doomed to return with every tide, to relive the dreadful events of 31 August 1936 and then go back to rest in the depths of the ocean, the symbol of the first womb. Behind Olivia are the voices of all her female ancestors, who try in vain to protect her from the lust of Stevens by warning her again and again not to trust him. In fact, Olivia and the men in her family do not trust Stevens, but no-one could anticipate the violence of which he showed himself to be capable. The chorus of women's voices whispering in the background give voice to the mistrust between men and women which is one of the underlying themes of the book. These women had learnt by bitter experience what to expect from men, and they recognise the danger in Stevens. The threat posed to women by men is made explicit in their warnings.

The symbolism, which plays so important a role in the book, operates on more than one level, but much of it is concerned with sex and the divide between women and men. The sexual symbolism of the gannets as they dive into the sea from a great height, their long sharp beaks thrusting down into the water, is clear. Their energy and strength represent the power of the male, while the ocean which receives them into its hollows with its softness and its wetness yields before them as the woman receives the man. The ocean is specifically identified with the female characters in the book. Its role as the source of life is brought out by Nora, the most optimistic character and the only one in Griffin Creek who seems to have any *joie de vivre.* Women are also identified with the weaker animals, the prey of the hunter who is usually seen as male. Men are linked to the wind, violent, unpredictable and dangerous, but unable permanently to tame or dominate women, just as neither they nor the wind can ever tame the sea. As a result, men and women are forever in conflict. The bleakness of the setting and the harshness of the climate symbolise the deeply pessimistic scrutiny that men and their harsh treatment of women receive at the hands of the author.

Chapter Three

Sexuality

As a small and isolated community, remote from centres of government or population, the people of Griffin Creek have turned inwards. They have married within the community, with the inevitable risk of inbreeding. Thus Olivia and Nora are first cousins through both their mothers and their fathers. Stevens is their first cousin through his mother, Bea, and all three mothers are the sisters of Nicolas Jones, the pastor. All the families have intermarried, and both language and religion cut them off from the outside world. Accustomed to a hard life of farming and fishing, the men are full of energy which it is difficult to control, and of which the women are the victims. The release for this energy takes the form of hunting or sex, and, as the village seems to be full of young people either already into adolescence like Nora, or young manhood like Stevens, Patrick and Sidney, sex naturally occupies much of their thoughts. It is not only the young people who have this on the brain, however. The opening narrative by the pastor makes it clear that the sexual practices of the men of the village have had a major role in shaping the attitudes within the community. In particular, the gap between the men and the women can be attributed in large part to the behaviour of the men.

The pastor comments on the large size of the immigrant families over the two centuries since they first settled in Griffin Creek, and later he comments on how the men of the village go hunting, and on their return make love to their wives in the dark without even taking their boots off: 'De retour de chasse ils prennent leur femme dans le noir, sans enlever leurs bottes' (**40**). He has to admit that he is of their race, like them hard and fierce and a devotee of the hunt:

> voici que je n'en finis pas de retourner à la terre originelle et d'être l'un d'eux, parmi eux, mes frères sauvages et durs. (**40**)

It is in this violence and thirst for blood that he sees the misfortune of Griffin Creek. The community is doomed, and Stevens will be the one responsible for bringing about its downfall, but all the guilt does not lie with him.[1] The pastor has always longed for the love of his mother, which was reserved strictly for her daughters and their

---

[1] Senécal. p. 157: 'Even though the apocalypse of the summer of 1936 is prepared by two centuries of dissoluteness, it is the sacrilege of the Reverend Jones that precipitates the days of violence and depravity that climax with the last night of summer, a maelstrom of murder and rage.'

daughters. His frustrated affection shows pronounced oedipal tendencies (Sirois, p. 181). Excluded by his sex from her morning bathes, he yearns to be accepted by her, but the only time that he even approaches achieving this is when he tells her that he has decided to become a minister. For once she clasps him to her bosom, but even then the pins stuck into the upper part of her dress keep him at bay (25). Later in life he longs for a child to present to his mother, a male child, who, he is sure, will replace Nora and Olivia in her affections. Vicariously he will achieve the recognition and enjoy the affection for which he has always longed. Even in this he is thwarted, for his wife, Irène, is barren and cannot bear him children despite the frenzy of his love-making. Frustrated and repressed, the pastor, who is only in his thirties, becomes obsessed with his niece Nora, and to a lesser extent, his other niece Olivia, spying on Nora like a voyeur when she bathes with her grandmother, flaring into jealousy when other men show an interest in her, and finally groping her in the boathouse. He is seen by Perceval, who runs away in distress to tell Irène, a disclosure that is swiftly followed by her suicide.

The responsibility can be taken one generation back, however, as the frustration of the pastor which is caused by lack of maternal affection, can be explained by the behaviour of his father. Felicity, his mother, has been nauseated by her treatment by his father, who not only fathered many legitimate children onto Felicity, but was also the father of many illegitimate children through a series of flagrant affairs starting in the first year of their marriage. Felicity can never forgive him or any other man for this treatment, and seeks refuge in her hour of peace at dawn, when she seems to reign over the sea and where no men can disturb her. Only as her husband, Peter, decays with the onset of old age and can no longer humiliate her with his sexual escapades, does Felicity begin to live and appreciate the life around her. The genetic inheritance offered to Peter's descendants is therefore distinctly unpromising, and Nicolas and Stevens both illustrate different perversions.

Nicolas, frustrated and lustful, becomes a voyeur and is drawn to incest. Stevens, however, is much more dangerous. He is obsessed with sex and also seems to be unusually attractive to women. He tells old Mic that on his way north back to his homeland from Florida, he worked at fish-gutting because the smell lingered and that alone could deter women from pestering him. He is no sooner back in Griffin Creek than he seduces his much older cousin, Maureen Macdonald, a widow who is longing for a man and whom he then treats with casual cruelty. He is drawn to Olivia, for whom even as a little boy he seems to have had a liking, and she is well aware of his attraction, although determined to resist. Olivia is well protected,

however, and her menfolk take care never to leave her alone with
Stevens. He exercises his spell on Nora, who is drawn to him partly
out of rivalry with Olivia, partly because he is an unknown quantity,
almost a stranger after five years absence, and she is not attracted by
any of the boys available. As soon as she starts to pursue him,
however, and even when she manoeuvres an ideal opportunity for
her seduction, he resists and spurns her. Sex is only interesting for
him when it is difficult. If the woman makes it too easy, then Stevens
is repelled. He accepts also the customs of the village. Unmarried
girls were sacrosanct: boys had to marry them or resort to the
guidounes or whores along the coast, which Stevens does in company
with his cousin Patrick and their friend Bob Allen, because, as Nora
shrewdly realises, he enjoys the low life.

> Stevens va à la ville de temps en temps, avec Bob Allen et Patrick.
> Pour les mêmes raisons que Bob Allen et Patrick. C'est ma mère qui me
> l'a dit. Je prétends que Stevens n'aime pas les femmes mais seulement
> la cochonnerie qu'on peut faire avec les femmes. (**130**)

His sexual drive is great, but he is not driven by any affection for
women. Sex is rather a means of dominating and degrading them.

It is possible that Stevens is actually a repressed homosexual,
whose hatred for women is an expression of his frustrated desire.
Homosexuality in a narrowly traditional community like Griffin
Creek in the 1930s would be wholly unacceptable, but Stevens has
been to Florida where he lived with his friend Mic. Mic's full name
is Michael Hotchkiss, and Hébert has stated that she picks the names
of the characters in her books with great care. The choice of
surname could therefore be very significant, hinting at a passionate
relationship between the two men. For Stevens, sex is linked with
violence, as in his memories of the war after his departure from
Griffin Creek, when he remembers the screams of girls being raped
by the light of explosions and to the sound of gunfire. Like his
uncle's, his sex drive takes a dangerous and unpleasant form.

Stevens's younger brother, Perceval, is just entering into puberty
at the age of fifteen and, although mentally handicapped, he is subject
to the same lusts as his older male relations. Like his uncle Nicolas,
he creeps down to the beach to watch Felicity and her
granddaughters bathing. He too is attracted by the budding sexuality
of Nora, and when the opportunity arises he fondles her in a way
that would get him severely punished if he were detected. Nora,
however, shelters him from the wrath of his father, John, who is a
cruel and dangerous man, joining with the twins Pam and Pat to
protect Perceval as far as they can from the cruelty of the adult
world. Perceval is filled with longings that he cannot express, and is
constantly watching his girl cousins. That is why it is Perceval who

discovers Nicolas pawing Nora in the boathouse; overwhelmed with grief at what he sees as the defilement of his cousin, he rushes away howling to alert his aunt Irène. Similarly at the barn dance, when he sees the pastor kissing the hands of Nora and Olivia, he bursts into tears because he thinks that the pastor wants to eat their hands. Only his grandmother can calm him, explaining that the pastor is not a girl-eating monster but a poor man driven by demons. Felicity understands her son only too well.

The girls are also aware of their growing sexuality. Olivia, who has been entrusted to her father and brothers by her dying mother and who promised her mother that she would be an obedient daughter, has been aware for years of the attraction of Stevens. She remembers scenes on the beach when they were little which showed that he was already aware of her.

> Le voici qui s'accroupit sur le sable tout à côté d'elle. Examine les pâtés de sable. Examine la petite fille. Ne sait qui il admire le plus ou du sable posé en tas bien alignés ou de la petite fille elle-même qui a construit tout ça. (**205**)

Her spirit recalls memories of him as a little boy, before he became dangerous but already in conflict with his father, foreshadowing the fight which will drive him from home at the age of fifteen. When he returns, he is an adult and almost a stranger, who attracts her and makes her uneasy simultaneously. She hungers for him to make her a woman, which would enable her to understand the mysteries of life.

> La science du bien et du mal n'a pas de secret pour lui. Si seulement je voulais bien j'apprendrais tout de lui, d'un seul coup, la vie, la mort, tout. Je ne serais plus jamais une innocente simplette qui repasse des chemises en silence. L'amour seul pourrait faire que je devienne femme à part entière et communique d'égale à égale avec mes mère et grand-mères... (**216**)

Her pride keeps him at bay.

> S'il me voyait rougir devant lui, à cause de lui qui me tourmente, une fois, une fois seulement et je mourrais de honte. (**217**)

This only increases the attraction for him, but he cannot catch her. Even when she is at her most vulnerable, just emerged from the water after swimming, she is as slippery as a fish or a mermaid. Before he can subdue her or win her over with his 'propos galants un peu bizarres' (**97**), Patrick emerges to defend his sister, and there is a savage battle between the two cousins.

All through the summer Olivia is obsessed with Stevens and dreads his departure for Florida. She is jealous of her cousin Nora, and their sexuality drives apart two girls who are described as 'jumelles siamoises' at one point, although they are actually of different ages. Olivia does not share the joyous optimism of Nora, as she is both drawn to and repelled by the thought of sex. She longs to be initiated, and her thoughts are concentrated on Stevens, but all her female ancestors warn her against him. In the end his sexual desire is too strong for her and destroys her, at a time when she had thought herself safe in the company of her cousin.

Nora is two years younger than Olivia, still at school, but obviously growing up fast. The boys are starting to notice her; Bob Allen and Patrick both kiss her, although she is not greatly impressed by either of them. A passing American is attracted to her by her vibrant youthfulness, and she responds enough to enrage her uncle, the pastor, who slaps her. He is attracted to her to the point where he can scarcely control himself, and Nora is well aware of her attractiveness. The man she wants to attract is Stevens, for a variety of reasons. She is jealous of her cousin, as she has realised that Stevens is far more interested in the remote and unattainable Olivia than he is in Nora. She is drawn to Stevens because of his undoubted appeal to women, and he is someone new and different. Nora was only eleven when he left Griffin Creek, and she would have only vague memories of him. He has been outside the region and is a change from the local boys to whom she is not attracted. She fantasises about her future husband, dreaming of a prince who will take her to some idyllic place. She prays that her first experience will be with someone attractive, not with any of the obvious candidates, Bob, Patrick or her uncle. She pursues Stevens, to the extent of following him through the forest. In her mind the traditional roles are reversed. She is the huntress and he the prey, until at the last moment, when he turns to confront her, she is overcome by weakness. To her fury she realises that he is the stronger, and that she has become the prey again. She resents this role as she yearns for equality in love, something that is wholly alien to most of the men of Griffin Creek. Rebuffed by Stevens, who is not attracted to women who pursue him, she allows herself to be fondled by her uncle, who is then racked with guilt after they are seen by Perceval.

Nora is experimenting with her sexuality. She is pretty and knows it. Her mother tries to make her father admit it, but he refuses. Subconsciously he is aware that her beauty is dangerous to her, and he tries to protect her from the risks of her attractiveness to men, ordering her home as soon as Sidney starts to show an interest in her at the hunt. She looks forward to experiencing 'le fun de tout mon corps' (**131**), marriage and motherhood, planning a large family. Confident in her attractiveness, she has no fear of men and wants to use her sexuality to control them. Her innocence and her confidence, however, mean that she is unable to calculate the effect that she is having on Stevens, and she dies before she has learnt all the things that she wants to know and experience.

Nora is the only character who does not associate sex with cruelty, guilt, pain or violence. For her, love with an attractive boy and 'fun' are exciting and alluring prospects which she is sure will come to her soon. She enjoys her femininity and looks for a love in which men and women will be equal. Perhaps this is because she seems to come from a happier home than any of the other characters. She is, of course, one of a large family, but her father and mother seem to be kind and still fond of each other as well as their children. She is longing for the return of her eldest brother, who is a pilot on the St. Lawrence, and has promised her exciting gifts of perfume and soap for her birthday. Her mother can tease her father, and her father in turn teases his daughters, although now that Nora is a young woman he is more restrained and turns his teasing to her younger sister, Linda. No one else has that sort of home life. Stevens, Perceval and the twins are the children of a harsh and brutal father, who beats the boys savagely for the slightest offence. Their mother is cold and unloving, for which Stevens cannot forgive her. Nicolas feels rejected by his mother, Felicity, who reserves all her love for her daughters and granddaughters. This rejection by their mothers means that both men harbour a bitter resentment against women, expressing itself in Nicolas's disgust when he gives in to temptation and in Stevens's contempt for women. Stevens wants to make women suffer and in the end, of course, does so, when he murders the cousins and rapes Olivia. Love is associated with pain and violence for the men of Griffin Creek. For the pastor it is sordid and unlovely. His lust for Nora is a sin. His intercourse with Irène, who resembles a dead fish (23-4), brings him no pleasure, especially when she fails to conceive. For Stevens, sex is a way of humiliating women and of asserting his dominance over them. He enjoys tormenting them, refusing to sleep with Maureen when she wants him to, but tantalising her by making love to her from time to time when he feels like it. He dreams of humiliating Olivia and all the other women in the village. His mother has made him incapable of loving any woman without making her suffer.

Sexuality in Hébert's vision is a dark and sinister force, driving a wedge between the dominant males and the submissive females. There are strong suggestions of sadism and perversion in the behaviour patterns of the men of Griffin Creek, and Nicolas Jones implies that these are deeply rooted in the community. Most of the women silently acquiesce, and almost masochistically accept their fate, thereby becoming accomplices in the downfall of a community.

Chapter Four

Non-narrators

Through the voices of her narrators, Hébert pieces together for her readers the characters who participate in the events of 1936 and shows them as they appeared to themselves and to others. The narrators are the major characters and will be looked at separately, but it seems preferable to begin with the characters who, although not insignificant, can at least be designated minor in the sense that they are not given their own distinctive narrative voice.

Maureen Macdonald is one such. A widow approaching fifty but still attractive with her black hair shot with silver, she is leading an apparently pleasant but empty life when Stevens descends on her cottage one morning in July. As a widow she needs an odd job man to do the rough work for her and she is able to pay. The sight of Stevens, still caked with the dirt of the road, long-legged and clearly now a man, overwhelms her. She cooks her breakfast for him and watches him devour it with pleasure. She insists on helping him to bathe and is overcome by the attraction of his sexuality, like so many other nameless women he has encountered in the States. In effect she offers herself to him, hungry for a man after years of widowhood, and the discovery that she is still attractive enough to seduce him revitalises her. Her cousins notice that she is taking immense care over her hair. She has taken to wearing more make-up, and Stevens sees that she is becoming sleek and contented. Her attraction is ephemeral, however. Stevens will not share her bed, but sleeps in the outhouse like any ordinary hired man. His love-making becomes more and more intermittent, and only at the times of his choosing.. Appearances are preserved, and the village is not scandalised, although the implication is that Maureen is so overcome with love that she would have been prepared to take that risk.

The affair quickly becomes a form of torture for her (Senécal, p. 156). Stevens is attracted by his younger cousins and has no wish to be attached to Maureen, except on his own terms. She is told that she is old. She is warned that at the end of August he will leave to go back to Florida. Her cousins notice that she trembles and suffers from hot flushes. She is probably experiencing the menopause, and may be prone to the emotional turbulence which affects some women. The disappearance of the two girls on their way home from her house is a terrible blow to her; she is barely able to move or to support herself. Whereas at the funeral of Irène she was able to be active and supplied from her garden all the flowers that the pastor could wish for, she is virtually paralysed by the deaths of her young cousins. Suddenly she becomes really old, clinging numbly to the fact that the girls left her house at nine-thirty. Her Indian summer is over, as the summer itself is drawing to a close, and she has little left to live for.

Good-hearted and vulnerable, Maureen suffers cruelly as Stevens takes his revenge on all women through her. She is an easy victim as, alone and hungry for love, she cannot conceal her longing for him. Briefly she finds happiness in their affair, but she is quickly made to see that she cannot compete with the younger women. She suffers because she is kind and generous, and she has no weapons with which to fight back. She is too much part of the tradition of Griffin Creek, where the women wait upon and serve the men. Stevens will abuse her readiness to conform, and treats her with a casual cruelty which is all the more insulting because for him it has so little importance. Although she does not physically die with Nora and Olivia, Maureen suffers a living death in which the suffering is prolonged. Her grief and misery make her a tragic figure and just as much one of the victims of Stevens's cruelty as the girls he killed.

Felicity, on the other hand, is not a victim of Stevens. She has reacted to her husband's multiple infidelities like 'une reine offensée' (34) bearing him many children from their presumably loveless couplings and reserving her love for her female descendants. For Felicity, men are intruders from whom she escapes to the loneliness and security of the sea, where she can be herself, at peace with the world. Once the dawn is over and she has to return to everyday life, she resumes her mask of cold competence, keeping her husband and sons at bay, even Nicolas, who desires nothing more than to earn her affection. Efficient and unemotional, she copes effortlessly with her household tasks, as can be seen on the morning after the disappearance of her granddaughters, the creatures for whom she cared most in the world. Despite the alarms and panic all around her, she produces breakfast for many people without fuss or hurry:

> Elle s'ingénie à rester pareille afin que rien d'autre ne change à Griffin Creek [...]. Elle a seulement mis plus de bois que d'ordinaire dans le poêle, fait un plus gros feu, une plus grosse pile de toasts, sorti de l'armoire la grande cafetière, préparé deux bonnes douzaines d'œufs et plusieurs paquets de bacon. (154)

Like many women, she finds some consolation for her unfaithful husband in religion. One of the rare occasions when Nicolas Jones earns his mother's unqualified approval is when he tells her that he has decided to become a minister. She kisses him for the first time, but even then he cannot get close to her, although he almost faints in ecstasy if her hand so much as touches his. Her coldness causes her

son great unhappiness, making him feel that he is excluded not only
from her love, but also from the secrets of women. This he resents,
as he watches her initiate her granddaughters into the joys of the sea,
her domain. As her husband sinks into senility and incontinence,
Felicity seems to dominate the family, but she is a remote,
unwelcoming matriarch. To her granddaughters she seems a majestic
figure: 'Mais voici ma grand-mère, de pied en cap, plus grande
encore que Perceval, plus forte que Perceval, la puissance même de
ce monde...' (**117**). She does not seek to alter things now that she has
freedom. Instead she remains aloof and uninvolved, although she is
perceptive and knows her children. She understands the demons that
torment Nicolas, as she explains to Perceval. Greatly wronged
herself, she wittingly or unwittingly inflicts great damage on her
male descendants. She is partly responsible for the unhappiness that
lies over Griffin Creek.

Irène is indirectly a victim of Felicity's coldness. She seems to be
an almost passive person, cold and dull like a fish. Her nieces think
that she is almost lifeless. There is no colour to her. She wears beige.
She refuses to dance at the barn dance, although her husband is
swinging his nieces round the floor. Her husband finds her physically
unattractive, and cannot forgive her sterility as this has destroyed his
hopes of gaining his mother's affection through his children. He had
hoped that his son would replace Nora and Olivia in the affections of
his mother, but in vain. Irène seems not to notice what is happening
around her, but she understands the babblings of Perceval when he
runs to tell her what he has seen in the boathouse. She shows no
immediate reaction to the news of her husband's attempted infidelity,
but when the chance comes in the small hours of the morning while
Nicolas sleeps, she quietly slips into the barn and hangs herself with a
rope specially bought for the purpose. Despised, rejected and
betrayed, she has the courage to end her life, leaving her husband
racked with double guilt for his near-betrayal of her and for her
death. She is a woman who has failed in every aspect of a woman's
life, and when this is made clear to her by her husband turning to
younger women, she has no desire to go on living. Irène suffers for
Felicity's coldness to her son, who cannot forgive Irène for failing to
let him win his mother's affection. Like Maureen, she is a victim of
the men of Griffin Creek. Unlike Maureen, she retains the capacity
to act and to put an end to her suffering, and by so doing she secures
some small measure of revenge.

Irène's sister-in-law Bea, like Felicity, has a damaging effect on
her son. Bea is cold and unloving, so cold that Stevens claims that he
was cold in her womb (**86**). She seems incapable of loving any of
her children, conceived and born reluctantly, endured rather than
loved. She makes no move to see Stevens when he returns to the

village, waiting for him to come and visit his parents. Only when there is trouble, and the police arrive to investigate the murders of Olivia and Nora, does Stevens return to his parents' home so that the family and the village can present a united front to the outsiders.

Her husband, John, is a cruel, harsh man who beats his children savagely. Nora knows as a little girl that things must be concealed from Uncle John—'Le visage de mon oncle John est maussade comme d'habitude' (114)—as otherwise he will make Perceval suffer. He is cruel to Stevens, a wilful and tough little boy whom he is determined to crush. He fails to break his spirit, however, and when Stevens is fifteen, there is the inevitable clash between father and son which becomes violent. Bea is unable to intervene, and Stevens leaves the house to drift for five years in the States. He does not regard himself as beaten by his father, and when he returns the older man has to accept that his son is now definitely the stronger.

This family is destroyed by the events of 1936, as Stevens is removed to prison and never returns to the village. Perceval is unhinged by the events, and his crying unnerves his parents so that they cannot bear to have him near them. He is sent away to the asylum, and his twin sisters Pam and Pat are dispatched to the parsonage to act as housekeepers to the parson.

> John et Bea Brown ayant mis au monde Stevens, Perceval et les jumelles, s'en sont débarrassés, au cours d'un seul été. (21)

The parents are happy to be rid of their unwanted children, for whom they feel no affection. According to Nicolas Jones this has long been their ambition: 'Réalisation d'un vieux rêve enfin justifié. Ne plus avoir d'enfant du tout' (21). They have produced four damaged children, for the twins, although not as mentally unstable as Perceval, are to some extent mentally handicapped.

> Ces filles sont folles. Non complètement idiotes comme leur frère Perceval, ni maléfiques comme leur autre frère Stevens, mais folles tout de même. Niaiseuses de manières. (17)

The heredity of the brutal, violent father and the cold, unloving mother results in children who are seen to be a menace to society (Hillenaar, p. 7). It is implied that two centuries of inbreeding are having their effect.

The twins function almost as one unit and much of the time are indistinguishable, from which they derive considerable satisfaction. Only when one of them scalds her hand is the parson able to tell them apart and even then he does not always bother. He is not interested in them as women, but simply as the creatures who see to his comfort. They are ruled with a rod of iron by the parson and lead narrow, cloistered lives in which they tend his house, care for him and obey him in everything. In their own way they are the victims of the men of Griffin Creek, exchanging a cruel father for a harsh, uncaring employer. Nonetheless they are not wholly subdued, for when the pastor decides to create his gallery depicting his ancestors right back to the first couple to settle in Griffin Creek, he entrusts to the twins the task of depicting the women. To his fury he finds that they have taken advantage of this opportunity to introduce some colour into their lives, adding a riot of flowers and brightly coloured hats and dresses to what he had intended to be a sober recreation of their ancestors. Lacking models, and somewhat in the manner of the portraitist of the kings (and queen) of Scotland whose works are displayed in Holyroodhouse, the twins use the faces of Nora, Olivia and Irène for their ancestresses revealing that the events of 1936 have not been forgotten by them. Into their work they also scroll a motif of 'étéétéétéété 1936193619361936' (**17**; **23**), a date which the pastor has been trying to bury.[1] Thus, subtly they disrupt his overall plan and introduce a note of feminine subversion, even in 1982 when they are two elderly, fading women, wholly dependent on him. Reluctantly the pastor has to recognise that they have a secret life from which he is excluded, just as he was excluded from the life of his mother and her granddaughters. He is even more astonished to find the twins showing a brief flicker of revolt when he closes the gallery and sends them back to the house. They want to keep the pots of coloured paint and the brushes which had so delighted them. The twins continue the tradition of females conspiring successfully to exclude men from certain parts of their life, even if men dominate them in other ways.

The young men of the village, Patrick and Sidney, the brothers of Olivia, and Bob Allen from the next village, are shadowy characters. They drink with Stevens and go to the brothels with him. They flirt with Nora, on whom they make no great impression, and Patrick and Sidney mount guard over Olivia. They have good reason to be suspicious when Stevens is in the village, but their motives are not entirely altruistic. Olivia keeps house for her father and brothers since the death of her mother, and is in many ways a prisoner. Her mother had not been happy. The brothers swore too much and took to drinking, impatient to escape from the protection of their mother's love. Their father encouraged them, anxious no doubt to have two manly sons who conformed to the Griffin Creek male norm. He has his wish: Sidney is a hunter, Patrick a superb

---

[1] Rea, p. 176: 'the details in their painting show, I think, that these little, aging women know much more about the summer's deaths than they have revealed in words.' Rea may well be right but if so, Hébert did not choose to develop this idea at all in her novel. It remains, at most, a tantalising hint.

swimmer, and both can drink. Patrick and Stevens empty a bottle of
smuggled liquor between them after Stevens has surprised Olivia at
her ironing. The implication of the mother's sadness is that Olivia's
father has been cruel to her mother, and the ghost of Olivia
remembers her mother's unhappiness. Not long before her mother's
death Olivia discovered blue marks on her arms and shoulders which
her mother had always tried to conceal from her. It is possible that
her husband beat her and that these marks are fading bruises.
Nonetheless the men are distressed when she dies and carry out
faithfully her dying injunction to 'veiller sur la petite' (**209**). When
Olivia disappears while staying with her aunt and uncle, they are
distraught and throw themselves frenziedly into the search for her,
but to no avail. Their affection seems real enough, but they are
rough and inconsiderate, like many young men who are trying to
prove themselves. After Olivia's death the house is abandoned, so
that when the ghost returns, she finds it deserted, a symbol of the
destructive effects of the events of 1936.

Alice and Ben Atkins, the parents of Nora, appear to be happily
married. They have a large family who seem to be happy and of
whom they appear fond. Gestures, such as Alice warning Nora to
beware when she goes into wood with food for the hunters or Ben
sharply sending Nora home when he sees the reactions of the pastor
and Sidney to her presence, show the care and attention given to the
children. An idea of their joyful family life is conveyed by the scene
in which Alice teasingly tries to make Ben say that Nora is pretty,
but he will not do so, for fear of making her vain (**134**).
Nonetheless, Nora suspects that he really thinks that she is pretty.
Alice is the first to give the alarm on the night of the disappearance.
As a loving mother, she gets worried when the girls do not return
from visiting Maureen. They are the only couple in Griffin Creek
described by Hébert to live happily together and whose children
seem to have the confidence and security that a loving upbringing
can provide. It is ironic that it is the very confidence which they
have instilled in Nora which leads to her death.

The only outsider individualised in the book is the detective
McKenna, chosen to investigate the crime because he is an
Anglophone. He is completely alien to the village and, through
Perceval's eyes in particular, is painted as a disagreeable and
unattractive man: 'Cette puanteur de policier est assise en face du
pasteur' (**163**). Physically he is repulsive, with his body odours and
clothes which are none too clean. He and the other policemen haunt
the village, introducing fear and apprehension into a community
which is already deeply scarred by the disappearance of the two
attractive teenagers. McKenna is no fool, however, and Perceval
soon realises that the two prime suspects are Stevens and Bob Allen.

Allen, however, has an alibi which cannot be broken, although the police try very hard, and this leaves Stevens as the chief suspect. McKenna sets out to break him and to extort from him a confession, which he does by using unacceptable methods, although little actual physical violence. There is mental if not physical third degree, but after the interrogations Stevens is like a zombie. McKenna gets the confession which he wants, only to see the judge rule it out of court, because it was not obtained legally. The irony is that, when he has escaped from the hospital and is writing his last letter to Mic, Stevens confirms that the confession was true, and that therefore McKenna was right all along. Justice has not been seen to be done because of the inadequacy of the humans chosen to uphold it. The failure to investigate according to the rules meant that the guilty party walked free. McKenna, an unclean, disagreeable bully, is another of the unattractive Anglophone males to be found in the book.

Chapter Five

Narrators

There are five main characters, all closely related. Stevens and Perceval are brothers, and they are the cousins of Nora and Olivia, who are themselves double cousins: 'cousines germaines par les mères et par les pères' (37). Nicolas Jones is uncle to all of them, and all three men are psychologically damaged.

Perceval Brown

The younger of John and Bea's boys is more than that, however. He is mentally handicapped, and further troubled by his awakening sexuality as he moves from childhood to adolescence. In fact he is almost a young man and very large; as Nora observes: 'Mon cousin Perceval grandit et grossit à vue d'œil. Il devient un géant' (116). She may be small, but her observation is supported by the searchers, who can no longer bear to have Perceval amongst them, screaming and shouting:

> Quelqu'un d'autre fait remarquer que «cet enfant» a quinze ans et qu'il est fort comme un bœuf. (153)

He is keenly interested in his cousin Nora, and when they are alone together, he clumsily tries to fondle her: 'Ses mains pataudes cherchent ma peau sous ma robe' (117). One morning he catches her after her swim and, throwing her to the beach, tries to mount her, but is prevented by the arrival of Felicity, who, in a voice that brooks no opposition, orders Perceval away and sends Nora home. Nora would not have reported the scene, but Felicity tells her son-in-law, and the consequences for Perceval are serious.

> Il ne fallait pas le dire à mon oncle John. Mon oncle John est méchant. Ma grand-mère a tout raconté et mon oncle John a battu Perceval avec un fouet comme on bat un cheval. (117)

The use of animal imagery is significant, because that is very much how Perceval is treated by his parents. He is locked up at night and allowed to run wild during the day, as long as he causes no trouble. As soon as he does, he is punished severely. Like Stevens, whom he admires, Perceval is acutely responsive to the weather. He adores the wind and is excited by the moon. On moonlit nights, after he has

been locked in, he likes to climb out of his window and explore by
the light of the moon. He loves to shout and scream when he is
excited, especially by the light of the moon (**139**), and this gets on
the nerves of all the adults in the community and leads to his parents
sending him away to the asylum when they can no longer bear his
noise and size. 'Cet enfant crie trop fort' (**153**) say the searchers for
Nora and Olivia, and they send him back to his parents where he can
be at peace in his bedroom, passing the time by innocently pleasuring
himself.

Perceval's narrative is preceded by a quotation from
Shakespeare's *Macbeth:* 'It is a tale told by an idiot, full of sound and
fury' (**137**). The quotation is incomplete, as Hébert has omitted the
concluding words of the sentence: 'signifying nothing', perhaps
implying the opposite. Perceval's tale is full of sound and fury, the
sound and the fury of the storm, of Perceval's own cries and shouts,
of the shouts of the searchers and the fury of the bereaved. It is full
of significance, for Perceval knows everything. His uncle Nicolas has
already said so in his narrative: 'Savait tout. Ne pouvait que gueuler'
(**20-21**). This is the tragedy of Perceval, that he can see and
understand but not communicate: 'Pas de mots pour dire l'effet des
merveilles dans ma tête. Déjà pour la vie ordinaire pas assez de mots'
(**140**). His name suggests that he is the holy fool of folk tale, who is
doomed to know the truth which others do not always recognise.[1]
When he does try to communicate the truth, it ends in tragedy. Irène
is able to understand his frenzied cries when he runs to her after he
has seen the pastor pawing the unresisting Nora in the boathouse.
The result of his ability to communicate is that Irène commits
suicide. At the time of the murder, however, Perceval does not try
to communicate. It is clear that he knows more than he is prepared to
say and that he is trying to bury this knowledge deep within himself.
He does not want to reveal what he knows, and the only conclusion to
be drawn is that he has seen Stevens commit the murder; Stevens,
whom he adores, because the man is kind to him and, insofar as he
can love anyone in his family, he does seem to love Perceval: 'Rêver
à mon frère Stevens qui est bon pour moi' (**142**).

Behind the ravings of Perceval there is the penetrating gaze of a
child who sees through adult hypocrisy. Perceval's tears at the sight
of his uncle kissing the hand of Nora are the justified reaction of
someone sensing danger, even though he translates it into fairy-tale
terms as an ogre eating the hand of a young girl. He has sensed the

---

[1] Francoli, p. 133: '*Perceval*, au regard et aux cris perçants, représente l'innocence, le bien, à
l'image du "Chevalier sans tache" du cycle breton dont il porte le nom.' She also points out in a
note on the same page that 'Perceval était déjà le nom du cheval quasi sauvage qui ne se laissera
pas dompter par la "grande Catherine" de la nouvelle "Le Torrent".' This is one of several examples
of intertextuality to be found in *Les Fous de Bassan*.

danger lurking inside Nicolas, which is then expressed more prosaically but equally clearly by Felicity, who reduces her son from an ogre to a poor man tempted by demons. Perceval will not admit what he saw on the night of the murder. He saw the foreign car and the boat out at sea, but then he returned to bed where he would be safe within the house of his parents. He hears his father summoned to go to help in the search and has to call from his locked bedroom to his mother to let his father back in. Her footsteps sound inexpressibly weary. Through the eyes of Perceval, the emotions of all the characters are revealed:

> Bob Allen a l'air complètement hébété. [...] Patrick a les yeux mauvais et la barbe bleue. [...] Elle-même [Maureen] debout, au milieu de la pièce, les bras le long du corps. Toutes ses forces rassemblées pour s'empêcher de tomber. (**148-9**)

The most profoundly affected, however, is Stevens, whom Perceval no longer recognises:

> Non, non ce n'est pas Stevens. Je ne le reconnais plus. Ce n'est pas lui. Il n'a plus son chapeau sur la tête. (**150**)

Perceval notices that he has just washed his face and hands and probably shaved, while his hair is freshly combed. Then Perceval is free to shout to his heart's content with the others as they search for the missing girls. Soon his shouting changes to a 'hurlement pur' (**151**) and, as the moon disappears, he fears that, in the grey hour of dawn, the searchers will never find Olivia and Nora. He seems to know that they are already the victims of the sea, as he fantasises that Felicity will appear, walking on the water, to produce them from the pockets of her dressing-gown. Breakfasting at his grandmother's house, he says nothing about the car or the boats which he has seen during the night because he is too frightened that he will be beaten for wanting to get out.

Later, he is the witness to the interrogation of Stevens by the fat policeman whom he would like to kill: 'Moi, avec mon petit couteau, bien racler tout le lard, jusqu'à l'os' (**158**). Because of his instinctive dislike of this foul-smelling man, Perceval is resolved to say nothing, but he listens as his parents, shrinking into themselves and not looking at each other, confirm Stevens's alibi, that he returned to the house towards nine o'clock. This has to be a lie, as the girls left Maureen's house at nine-thirty. When Perceval confides in Stevens that he has to hold his nose when the policeman comes to the house, he makes Stevens laugh and relax for the first time since the disappearance of the girls. He rubs Perceval's head in the way that he likes, just as he did before 31 August.

The policemen order that Perceval be released from the house so that he can run at will 'comme un chien' (again the comparison is made with an animal, suggesting that Perceval is less than wholly human), and he heads for the beach, sure that he can see Nora, like a flicker of flame running ahead of him until she is snuffed out like a candle. He comes back weeping, and the policeman tries to question him, but with scant success. Later he eavesdrops on the interview between the police and his uncle the pastor, who also returned home from the beach about nine o'clock, as confirmed by the twins. Pat, however, has something to tell, that she heard dreadful cries that night which she told herself must have been cats, but her remark leads nowhere. When Perceval returns to the beach, the migrating birds remind him that soon Stevens will leave for Florida like them, but this time his head will be unprotected as his hat is lost. He fears that no one will have pity on them as there is no one to intervene with God.

> Qui aura pitié de nous, pense Perceval, les mains jointes, les yeux comme gelés dans sa face ronde, qui pourra adoucir la terrible face de Dieu. (**170**)

He overhears his parents' stalling when interviewed again by the police, while Stevens has repeated himself so often that he no longer seems to believe it himself. Perceval has to escape to get rid of the nausea inspired by McKenna. He spies on Olivia's brothers and father, helpless in their fury at the loss of Olivia, and he hears Maureen tell the police that at ten to eleven on the night of 31 August, she saw a man whom she did not recognise come up the path from the beach to the road.

It is, of course, Perceval roaming the beach who discovers the bracelet, during a tiny lull in the wind which he claims to have experienced only once before, while he was still in the womb. Looking out of his mother's navel, he saw the day draw breath. It is the same when he discovers the bracelet. There is a momentary lull in the wind to mark the importance of the discovery. When he takes the bracelet home, it is passed from hand to hand in total silence, with each second becoming more and more sinister.

> L'absence de parole gêne d'autant plus que nos pensées à tous sont déjà mûres et volettent dans la pièce, ressemblent aux papillons de nuit autour d'une lampe. (**179**)

Perceval appreciates all too well the meaning of this silence: 'J'entends si fort ce que pensent mon père et ma mère que je me mets à pleurer. Le silence de Stevens' (**179**). Later he is with his father when the news comes in that the belt has been found, and goes with him and Stevens with desperate haste to retrieve it. Both belt and bracelet disappear, although Perceval knows that his father, who threw it into the stove, has burnt the belt. Nothing can be done about the way the coat turns up, however; this confirms that Nora must be dead and her body in the sea, as it is found by her father out on the beach with Perceval, and her cousin had foreseen that any other discovery would come from the sea.

After the discovery of the coat comes the storm, which lasts for three days, the east wind blowing without ceasing, sending the sea crashing onto the shore, stripping the trees of their leaves so that they look like winter trees, the harbinger of a disaster. As the sea is too rough for fishing, Perceval's father takes him to the beach to collect clams, but suddenly he stops, 'Plus courbé que jamais, ses cheveux en piquants drus sur sa tête on dirait un martin-pêcheur fasciné par sa proie, entre deux eaux' (**187**). The horror of this scene is emphasised by Perceval's own reaction.

> Je vois mais je comprends pas. Veux pas comprendre. Regarder seulement. Un malheur est arrivé à Griffin Creek et nous le regardons ce malheur... (**187**)

Perceval cannot accept that this half-eaten body is all that remains of Nora. The idea is too horrible. His sensitivity to what is happening around him is shown when McKenna comes back to question Stevens for the umpteenth time about the murder. Perceval detests this malodorous policeman, and hides under the staircase to hear what happens. He knows that Stevens has something to hide and is eager to prevent such a disaster. He fears for his brother.

> N'ont qu'une idée en tête. Prendre mon frère Stevens en faute. Le jeter tout vivant dans un de ces grands sacs de toile grise...(**193**)

Perceval's fraternal affection is greater than any other emotion, although he yearns also for his cousins. His thoughts are divided between Stevens, in prison in some distant city because McKenna has put words into his mouth, and his cousins, who are lost forever. Perceval has never accepted that the corpse washed up after the storm was Nora. For him his cousins are forever lost in the sea, and if he looks very hard at low tide where the sea meets the sky, he can see them glinting like silver fish, their laughter glittering in the light.

Thereafter Perceval disappears from the book. Olivia's ghost makes no mention of him as she sweeps through the dying village. Stevens refers to him once in his letter to old Mic, when he comments on Perceval's affection for him: 'C'est fou d'ailleurs ce que cet enfant m'est attaché. Ne me trahira jamais' (**243**). Stevens knew that he had much to hide and that Perceval could have betrayed him, but the bond between the two brothers, careless affection on the part of the elder, dog-like devotion on the part of the younger, was too strong for that. The reader already knows from the book of Nicolas Jones that Perceval was sent off to an asylum shortly after the events of 31 August, as his parents could not endure to have him near them any longer. Clearly the tragic events of the summer had unsettled his frail grip on reality still further, and his refuge in noise and shouting, coupled with his great size and strength, had become too much to endure. Parents lacking in warmth and affection had had no trouble in disposing of their unloved children. Poor Perceval, with his capacity for love and affection, his innocence and eagerness, who would have loved to escape from the harsh environment of Griffin Creek and go to Florida with Stevens, is instead locked away with the burden of his knowledge and his unhappiness. The simpleton is one of the most tragic and sympathetic characters in the book.[2]

Nicolas Jones

Perceval, the innocent, is a victim of the cruelty of his family and their impatient, violent natures. His uncle, Nicolas Jones, is the victim of his own nature as well as of his parents. Child of an unloving marriage in which his father regularly betrayed his mother and thus made her despise all men, Nicolas grows up desperate for the approval and affection of his mother. It is to win her approval that he decides to enter the ministry, and for once he succeeds in arousing a display of maternal affection and approval, but the moment of tenderness is short-lived. He bitterly resents the feeling that all her affection is reserved for her daughters, and ultimately for their daughters. His whole ambition is to father a son who will replace these females in the affections of his mother and secure the place which Nicolas feels is rightly his. There seems no reason why his ambition should ever be realised, as Felicity's affections are always directed towards her female descendants, something that Nicolas himself accepts. His desire for a son is the male desire to reproduce himself and his lineage. As Nicolas cannot do this, he has to turn to recreating his ancestors as a substitute. His hope that his son would replace his nieces in the affections of his mother looks like masculine self-deception.

Repeating the pattern of his parents, he has made a loveless marriage: he finds his wife unattractive. Nevertheless he persists in making love to her in his desperate search for a son.

---

[2] Randall, p. 79: 'Or le seul personnage qui soit clairement exonéré de cette culpabilité générale est Perceval, dont l'innocence est absolue en raison de son enfance éternelle.'

> pareille à un poisson mort, sa vie froide de poisson, son œil de poisson,
> sous la paupière sans cils, son odeur poissonneuse lorsque je m'obstine
> à chercher, entre ses cuisses, l'enfant et le plaisir. (23-4)

It is symbolic that his desire for a child comes before his quest for pleasure. The smell of fish, which Stevens had used to repel the over-amorous women who were attracted to him in the States, disgusts him. From childhood he has sought to please his mother. When he begged her to take him with her on her morning swims, he found her calmer and more placid than usual, although she would never permit him to come with her.

> Et moi qui suis tout petit sur le sable et elle si grande, je saute autour
> d'elle comme une sauterelle dans l'herbe. Je supplie.
> —Emmène-moi avec toi, me baigner avec toi...
> Ma mère dit non doucement ainsi qu'au sortir d'un rêve. Le reflet du
> rêve persiste sur son visage pacifié, s'attarde aux commissures des
> lèvres, lui donne l'air d'émerger d'un mystère joyeux. [...] Son visage
> se renfrogne un peu, puis devient tout à fait soucieux quand nous
> montons les marches du perron. (35-6)

As the sun rose and she drew nearer the house, however, she would withdraw into her usual cold, distant, reserved character, in which he could no longer awaken any spark of affection. When in her old age she invites her granddaughters to accompany her to the beach at dawn or even before, Nicolas is consumed with jealousy and, like Perceval, he spies on the trio in their female world from which the men are rigorously excluded.

He is driven not only by jealousy but by lust. Unsatisfied in his own marriage, which has brought him neither an heir nor real sexual pleasure, he is obsessed with his nieces, but in particular by Nora, who resembles him: 'Les deux les plus roux de Griffin Creek (comme des renards, dira Perceval)' (43). He has secretly watched them swimming with their grandmother, and he is all too aware of Nora's awakening sexuality. He sees immediately the interest which the visiting American takes in her, and senses that she is ready to respond. Two shots from his gun suffice to frighten off the American and leave him face to face with his laughing niece, who had disregarded his warning to be careful of strangers. He is provoked beyond endurance by repressed desire, which is so obvious to others that his mother has warned him about his behaviour: 'Tu la suis à la trace cette petite. Tu ferais mieux d'aller te faire la barbe et changer de linge' (41). He had become a hunter like the other men of the community, 'mes frères sauvages et durs' (40). The violence of all the men of Griffin Creek is just below the surface in Nicolas, poorly disguised by his clerical garb. It explodes when Nora laughs in his face, and he slaps her violently, revealing his true nature:

> Mon oncle Nicolas est une brute. Sous des dehors exquis, son col de
> clergyman, ses manières suaves, se cache une brute épaisse. **(119)**

Despite Nora's wish that neither he nor Perceval should be her first
lover, Nicolas gets another opportunity when Nora is in a furious
rage after being rebuffed by Stevens. Her uncle is unaware that she
allows him to approach her only to avenge herself on Stevens. He
draws her into the boathouse where he fondles her breasts, while
telling her, not untruthfully, how unhappy he is. How far they would
have gone is deliberately left unclear, as Perceval interrupts them,
although even he cannot mistake what is happening and runs to warn
Irène. Nicolas breaks away violently, accusing Nora of being evil
and bringing sin into Griffin Creek. He reverts instantly from
would-be seducer to clergyman, implicitly likening his niece to Eve,
who caused the fall of man.

In his own narrative he can no longer hide from his guilt. He has
to try to face the consequences of his lust. At night beside Irène, he
contemplates his sin in the boathouse, having had to face Irène at the
supper table and failed to sustain her gaze.

> Ma chevelure flamboyante posée sur ma face pâle comme une
> oriflamme je baisse les yeux sous le regard de cendre d'Irène Jones, ma
> femme. **(45)**

Perceval's warning had not seemed to affect Irène, who quietly told
him to go home, and Nicolas is confident that she had not really
understood what Perceval was saying, but when the opportunity
came, she silently left the bed which she shared with Nicolas and,
with a newly-bought rope, went out and hanged herself. Nicolas is
thus doubly guilty. Not only was he ready to be unfaithful to his wife
and actively seeking the opportunity to commit incest with his
beautiful niece, but the knowledge of his activities drove his wife to
suicide. For forty-six years he has had to live with this burden, that
he, who should have been removed from all these emotions, has been
one of the worst sinners and one of the sinners who has brought
unhappiness to others. He is aware of his failings as a man of God:

> Je surveille cet homme qui regarde Nora, au loin, sur la grève. Je le
> hais comme il n'est pas permis à un pasteur de le faire, entre tous les
> hommes. **(43)**

He is even a suspect, if only briefly, in the murder. He had been on
the beach on the evening of the murders, although he claimed to have
returned by nine o'clock. The police quickly lose interest in him,
concentrating on Stevens and Bob Allen as the two principal suspects,
but Nicolas's conduct has been sufficiently bizarre to leave the reader

with the uneasy feeling that he could easily have committed the murders, given the opportunity.

The death of Irène leaves a mark on him which can never be removed. His nieces notice immediately that his voice has changed. Before the death of Irène he had been noted for his beautiful voice, but at her funeral service, which he insists on conducting himself, his voice has altered: 'Mais sa belle voix n'était plus la même, toute cassée et râpeuse' (130). The voice symbolises the personality, and henceforth Nicolas withdraws into himself, presiding, as he later realises, over the disintegration of the village: 'Il a suffi d'un seul été pour que se disperse le peuple élu de Griffin Creek' (13). He turns for consolation to the Bible, in particular the prophets of the Old Testament, amongst whom his favourite is appropriately Malachi, the prophet who writes about the sins of the preachers, and tyrannises the twins, the sisters of Perceval and Stevens, his servants since they were young teenagers.

> J'aime les voir trembler quand je les réprimande, dans la cuisine, pleine de buée et de l'odeur persistante du linge bouilli. (17)

He takes pride in his strictness, which verges on cruelty when he summons them from their beds to minister to his needs even in the middle of the night, for Nicolas has great difficulty in sleeping. His task remains to preach Christianity to his dwindling community, reminding them of the world when it was innocent.

Griffin Creek was lacking in innocence even before the return of Stevens. The pastor is all too well aware of the violence and hatred in the community. In his own family there was no love between his mother and his father, and his mother had little love for her son. The men of the community are violent and harsh, in keeping with their environment. His brother-in-law John is violent and cruel to his children. His sister, Bea, John's wife, is cold and unloving. Nicolas Jones sees that the village is too inbred, and everyone knows too much about everyone else.

> Trop près les uns des autres. Ces gens-là ne sont jamais seuls. S'entendent respirer. Ne peuvent bouger le petit doigt sans que le voisin le sache. Leurs pensées les plus secrètes sont saisies à la source, très vite ne leur appartiennent plus, n'ont pas le temps de devenir parole. (30-31)

Although at the time he had accused Nora of bringing sin to Griffin Creek, in fact the pastor, with hindsight, knows that the catalyst for the events of the summer of 1936 was Stevens, who 'n'aurait jamais dû revenir' (31). The return of Stevens unleashed many of the

tensions which lay beneath the surface of village life (Sirois, p. 180)
and the pastor is aware that their destinies are inextricably entwined.

> Stevens est avec nous pour l'éternité et non plus seulement de passage
> pour un seul été [...]. Nous sommes ensemble, liés les uns aux autres,
> pour le meilleur et pour le pire, jusqu'à ce que passe la figure du monde.
> **(48)**

Although Stevens was the catalyst, Nicolas Jones sees himself as
the most guilty. Forty-six years after the dreadful events of 1936, he
waits for death to face the judgement of God, who alone can absolve
him of his guilt, for he considers that he is the true destroyer of the
community.

> *Un jour je connaîtrai comme je suis connu.* Tout sera clair dans la
> lumière du Jugement. Hors du monde je verrai tout Griffin Creek, de
> haut en bas et de long en large, comme un pays peuplé d'hommes et de
> femmes à l'âme vivante. Et je verrai Dieu, face à face, et ma faute sera
> sur ma face comme une ombre. Dieu seul pourra me laver de l'ombre de
> ma faute et tout Griffin Creek avec moi que je traîne dans l'ombre de ma
> faute. **(47-8)**

The Day of Judgement alone can give Nicolas peace of mind, since
he, chosen by God to be his servant, has failed so completely in his
task. He had prepared himself carefully for his career, learning by
heart the *Psalms* of David, practising how to project them against the
forces of nature. His mother, however, had seen the weakness in her
son, too proud of his beautiful voice: 'Mon fils s'écoute parler, pense
Felicity Jones' **(29)**. His narcissism can be sensed by others. For
Nora, God no longer speaks through the voice of her uncle:

> mais depuis quelque temps je n'entends plus la parole de Dieu dans la
> voix de l'oncle Nicolas. C'est comme si Dieu se taisait dans la voix de
> l'oncle Nicolas. La voix sonore de l'oncle Nicolas, sans rien de pieux
> dedans... **(30)**

Even before the disaster of 31 August, Nicolas is a lost sheep,
although he does not then realise it. Nearing death he can accept that,
as the one with the highest calling, his was the greatest failure.

With no future to look forward to for himself, or for the son
which he never had, he attempted to make his line everlasting by
creating a gallery of ancestors right back to Henry Jones, the
Loyalist who fled from Montpelier (Vermont) to land on this
desolate coast. For ten generations he traces the Joneses back through
history, creating his father's likeness from himself, his grandfather's
from his father's, and so on. In this way he feels the pride of
fatherhood, even if it is only these painted images who all look alike
apart from the colour of the hair which he varies according to his

whim.[3] He entrusts the painting of his female ancestors to the twins, who suddenly discover the pleasure of painting. Whereas the pastor had created grim figures, dressed sombrely in black with white shirts, the twins luxuriate in a riot of colour. Blue fish, red birds, purple seaweed adorn the walls, surrounding the heads of women in hats and ribbons;

> plus vivantes qu'aucune créature de songe hantant Griffin Creek depuis la nuit des temps. (16)

To the fury of the pastor, the twins include the heads of Nora, Olivia and Irène in their wall, 'malgré ma défense' (16), floating in a décor of sea grass, fishing nets, ropes and stones. Their names are inscribed here and there in the pictures, and round the wall runs a scroll of *1936,* and beneath it, a second line of *été.* The gallery is ruined in the pastor's eyes, and although it is unfinished, he banishes the twins from it, blaming himself for being so stupid as to entrust the work to two simpletons. Just like Perceval and Stevens, their brothers, the twins are crazy. They are not malevolent like Stevens, nor completely mentally deficient like Perceval, but nonetheless they are simple-minded, and the pastor eventually discovers that they are haunted by the events of 1936. To his surprise, he also discovers that, for all his years of dominance and his strict control of them, they can still take a malicious pleasure in defying him. When he banishes them from the gallery they want to keep their brushes and paints, and again the pastor is surprised at their protest. He has realised that even these apparently docile women can thwart and defy him. He has failed to leave a son to succeed him, and now the twins have frustrated his attempt to leave his own record of his ascendance. He is utterly sterile, pathetic in his impotence, dependent on the despised women to help him get out of his chair or go to bed. Nicolas Jones symbolises the failure of Griffin Creek.

Stevens Brown

If Perceval represents innocence and Nicolas Jones represents guilt, Stevens represents evil. Like his brother and sisters he has a bad inheritance, a cruel father and a cold, unloving mother.[4] He left

---

[3] This suggests that Hillenaar (p. 11) goes too far when he says: 'Ces livres si peuplés de grand-mères, d'Urmutter, jusqu'à la nième génération, ne connaissent guère d'ancêtres masculins, pas d'Urvater.' For one man at least his masculine ancestors do exist, although they are not a presence in the book in the way that Olivia's mother and female ancestors are.

[4] Senécal, p. 155: 'The seeds of evil come to full fruition with the generation of Stevens Brown but the arrival of this dark prince is prepared by a long lineage.'

the family home at the age of fifteen after a violent fight with his
father, when he resisted the beating which John Brown was about to
administer. When he returns at the age of twenty, he is the stronger,
and the father tacitly has to accept the change in their respective
status. When Stevens finally visits his parents, he can see from his
seat the spot in the kitchen where their bodies were entwined as they
fought, while his mother stood helplessly by. He has postponed as
long as possible the visit to his parents, to let them know indirectly
that he is independent of them and that the breach between is not
healed. Maureen is slightly shocked by his attitude, but accepts it
because she has succumbed so quickly to his sexual attraction.
Eventually social conventions are observed, and Stevens pays a
formal visit to his parents to re-establish contact with them. After the
murders he moves back into their house to form a united front
against the intrusions of the police.

Five years of travelling in the U.S.A. have left Stevens eager to
see his birthplace, although he firmly intends to return at the end of
the summer to Florida, where old Mic is waiting in the bungalow
next to the whitest sands in the world. At the sight of Griffin Creek,
Stevens realises that he has not abandoned his childhood with all its
joys and sorrows, and this unsettles him. His lack of confidence
momentarily makes him think of seeking out his grandmother,
Felicity, the only person to whom he would raise his hat, to ask for
absolution. This 'folle' idea is quickly dismissed. He contemplates
instead which house in the village to visit first, as his parents' house
will certainly be the last. For a moment his certainty wavers as he
wonders if he will be recognised, for if he is not, he will leave at
once to lose himself in the vastness of the continent. As he sits on top
of the hill looking at Griffin Creek beneath him, for an instant he
feels like a giant able to crush the tiny, distant village beneath his
enormous foot: 'Je joue à posséder le village et à le perdre à volonté'
(**63**). The threat posed by the arrival of Stevens is foreshadowed in
this scene before he descends the slope to begin the corruption of his
relations. He knows that, wherever he goes, his visit will be
immediately noticed, but Maureen's house is hidden amongst trees, it
is the first one in the village, and so he decides to start with this one.

Stevens belongs to the Canadian literary tradition of the
'Survenant', who arrives in some sleepy backwater for a temporary
stay.[5] When he leaves, nothing is the same. The difference from
Germaine Guèvremont's *Survenant* is that Stevens is not a beneficial
influence, but, as the pastor recognises and Nora senses, is evil.
Stevens is well aware of his own capacity for wrongdoing (Senécal,
p. 156). Olivia fears him even when she is attracted to him, and is

---

[5] Sirois, p. 181, also sees him as a parody of the Prodigal Son.

aware, whenever he is near her, that the ghostly voices of all her dead female ancestors are warning her against him. His attractiveness to women is remarkable. On his journey north to Griffin Creek he has to make himself unattractive by reeking of fish, to discourage the women who would otherwise be pestering him. Unshaven and covered in the dirt from the road, he still seduces his cousin Maureen without even trying. Thereafter she is completely besotted with him, and Stevens enjoys himself, controlling her, making her wait, and making love to her on his terms. He observes the proprieties and sleeps, like any ordinary hired man, in the barn, where he can masturbate in peace. He copulates with her only during the day between job, and even that less and less frequently. Maureen is all too well aware that she has rivals in the village in the shape of her nubile, teenage cousins, Olivia and Nora, and Stevens slowly tortures her by letting her see that he prefers the younger girls, reminding her that she is old and in the end announcing that he is leaving to return to Florida because of this. Despite his sexual attractiveness and his awareness of the effect he is having on his female cousins, Stevens respects the local conventions that a girl is sacred until she is married.

> Les filles d'ici sont intouchables jusqu'au mariage. C'est le pasteur mon oncle qui l'a dit. Tout le mal vient de là. Autant prendre son fun chez les guidounes et laisser les petites oies macérer dans leur jus. (**242**)

When he is bored with Maureen, he goes with his cousin Patrick and Bob Allen to the local brothels in the next town, behaviour which is, of course, noticed and commented on by his aunts and cousins but which is accepted as part of the normal behaviour for young men. Stevens knows that Nora and Olivia are interested in him, but he is able to control himself when Nora stalks him in the wood one day. They are quite alone, and she has placed herself in his power, but he provokes her by praising the beauty of Olivia. His intention is quite deliberate, because when Nora is enraged she sparkles with beauty. She rouses his curiosity by referring to Olivia's webbed foot, but when he accuses her of jealousy, she is insulted and takes flight, screaming her hatred for Stevens. His response is laughter.

He is in fact far more attracted to Olivia, who is much less available. She is guarded by her father and her two brothers, who rarely leave her unprotected. When Stevens arrives at the house to watch her ironing, she takes care to let him know that Patrick is asleep upstairs. When he catches her after swimming and tries to embrace her on the beach, begging to be allowed to see the webbed foot described by Nora, which fascinates him, Patrick quickly arrives on the scene to defend his sister, and there is a fierce fight between the two cousins from which neither emerges unscathed. He had always been drawn to her, even as a little boy. Olivia can remember a time when he allowed her to join in the boys' games, despite the impatience of her brothers and their juvenile contempt for females. She can also remember playing with Stevens on the beach, and seeing early signs of the conflict with his father which was going to drive him away from the village. Even as a small boy, Stevens had not feared his father and had resisted him to the best of his ability. Stevens haunts Olivia when he gets the chance, letting her see how interested in her he is, aware of her suspicions of him, trying to draw her into some show of interest in him. He even appears in the door of the church to watch the two Atkins cousins singing, but disappears again as soon as everyone has noticed him. Stevens represents something new and exciting in the village. He is slightly unusual because, although he is related to all of them, he has been away for five years, and the difference between the fifteen-year-old adolescent who left after fighting with his father and the tough, twenty-year-old man who has come back is sufficiently great to make him almost a stranger. He thus has the attraction of mystery and adventure, together with the physical allure already mentioned.

The other side of Stevens is one that he shares with Perceval: he loves the wind and the storms. During the storms he wanders in the wildest weather, shouting like Perceval, in answer to the forces of nature, feeling the great surge of the waves and the sweep of the winds. During the great summer storm which batters Griffin Creek, Stevens is out on the beach, revelling in the violence of the elements which answers the violence in his own nature. In the middle of the storm he makes his way to the house of Ben Atkins, the father of Nora, where Olivia is staying with her cousin, to beg Olivia and Nora to come out with him into the storm. His uncle thinks that he is completely drunk, but Nora realises that he is drunk with the excitement of the storm. He seems half out of his mind to his relations and refuses to stay with them, saying that he must go out into the storm again, which he does.

The half-controlled violence of Stevens bursts forth in its full fury on the night of 31 August, when he goes down to the moonlit beach with his cousins after the girls leave the house of Maureen Macdonald. Stevens, who has already planned his departure for Florida for the next day, is having as little contact with Maureen as possible, and so avoids going into the house with the girls. Instead he goes to the beach to bail out his boat and is waiting for the girls when they leave Maureen's.

Nora is still full of spite against him and, her temper rising as she looks at him with Olivia, she hurls insults at him, using the worst vocabulary of the fishermen of Griffin Creek, words which she did not know a couple of weeks earlier in the woods. She accuses him of not being a man, repeating the insult several times, her hysteria rising as she lashes herself into a fury. His masculinity is called into question by one of the sex he despises. To Stevens it feels as if the storm inside his mind is being matched by the fury of the elements, although everyone else will later swear that there had never been such a calm night in Griffin Creek. As Nora's fury rises, he feels the wind sweeping in from the sea and the storm beating against his temples from inside his head. Nora is small and slight, the murder is quickly performed, almost by accident, as he tries to quieten the torrent of abuse which strikes at his masculinity. She is dead before he has the time to enjoy himself: 'Pas eu le temps de jouir d'elle' (245). With Nora dead at his feet, in a position of supplication, he revels in the feeling of power over this woman who had challenged him. He admits quite openly to old Mic how much he enjoyed the sensation.

> Je te mentirais, old brother, si je n'insistais pas sur le fait que longtemps après Griffin Creek je me suis plu en cet agenouillement de Nora Atkins, ma cousine, devant moi, sur le sable. (245)

She haunts his life afterwards, appearing to him during the war, when he is in London during the Blitz, advancing through Normandy, where he committed rape and all sorts of other horrors, even in the hospital from which he has just escaped. He savours the thought that this woman's pride and scorn lie tamed and defeated at his feet.

At the time he has other things to think about, as Olivia immediately turns to flee up the cliff path to safety. She is brought down, raped and strangled, under the battering force of the wind:

> Et moi j'affirme avoir éprouvé la rage de la tempête dans tout mon corps secoué et disloqué, tandis qu'Olivia se débattait, partageant avec moi le même ressac forcené. Dans toute cette histoire, je l'ai déjà dit, il faut tenir compte du vent. (246)

The wind seems to be his ally, for he swears it is the wind that lifts the skirts of Olivia, the wind that drowns her cries as he tries to penetrate her. The wind lashes her skirts the way it had lashed the sheets on the clothes line on one of his visits to her house, when her brothers were mounting guard. He fights his way through her underwear, treating her like one of the whores that he has frequented in the brothels, and in his letter of 1982 contrasts her with the tarts of the rue Sainte-Catherine who wear nothing under their jeans. He is determined to possess her, to make her admit that her body is not perfect because of her pubic hair, to defile and degrade this girl who

is 'trop belle et sage' (**248**). Together with the noise of the storm
Stevens can hear the noise of the sea-birds. The gannets (*les fous de
Bassan*) whirl and scream above the three bodies on the beach and
return to haunt him every night thereafter. In the hospital he can feel
their beaks hammering at his skull and the noise of their wings
filling the room.[6] Everyone else will swear that the sea-birds never
stirred all night, but for Stevens the night of the murder is forever
linked with the violence of the storm and the noise of the birds.

The rape and double murder, which may or may not be
premeditated (Ewing, p. 107), are the final expresson of Stevens's
loathing and hatred for women.[7] The coldness of his mother and her
lack of interest in her children, the dominance of his authoritarian
grandmother, his harsh upbringing in a fiercely masculine
community, have all combined to leave him with a hostile and
contemptuous attitude towards women. They are there for his
convenience when he feels inclined to notice them. His attitude to
Maureen could not be more ruthless and unkind. He rouses her
sexually, making her realise that she is still a woman and not
unattractive, and then gradually makes her feel that she is in fact old
and that most pathetic of creatures, the older woman yearning for a
young lover. He talks of training her. He torments his young cousin
Nora, whose affection he does not really want, and murders her
when she turns against him and challenges, perhaps accurately, his
masculinity. He constantly seeks out his cousin Olivia, who does
attract him and towards whom he has in the past shown some
affection, but her beauty and her virtue become a challenge to him
which in the end he is only too ready to destroy to prove his own
superiority (Bishop, 'Distance', p. 120). He refers to the three
women as a bleating troop. All his thoughts about women reveal a
violent nature that despises them, as he shows on one of his first
visits to the house of Olivia: 'Cette fille est trop belle, il faudrait lui
tordre le cou tout de suite avant que...' (**79**). Olivia's voices are right
to warn her against Stevens, who represents a threat to all the women
in the community, except perhaps Felicity.

For one person only in Griffin Creek does Stevens feel any
affection and that is Perceval, but even this is a rather selfish
affection that does not cost him anything. He is kind enough to
Perceval, who receives so little affection that he naturally responds
to any that is offered. He confides in old Mic, but there is no
guarantee that the letters were ever sent or even meant to be sent,
making Mic really a substitute for himself. Stevens uses the letters

---

[6] Sirois, p. 182, sees here a clear parallel to the classical myth of Prometheus who was
tortured by an eagle.

[7] Rea, p. 176, argues, along similar lines, that Stevens fits the identikit description of the
rapist.

more as a sort of diary. He is intensely introverted, mentally unstable, and driven to the edge of sanity by the combination of the violent storm just before 31 August and the insults of Nora on the night of the 31st. These awaken the full force of his deep hatred of and contempt for women, and he takes his revenge on his two cousins, escaping justice only because of the methods used by McKenna to extract his confession. His mental condition is then aggravated by experiences in the war which confirm the violence and brutality of his nature, and finally he is confined in hospital for many years.[8] His life is destroyed, as he has destroyed the lives of Olivia and Nora, and these murders led in turn to the slow destruction of Griffin Creek, so that by 1982 it is tottering on the verge of extinction. Stevens represented evil in both its seductive and destructive aspects, and his family and relations were well aware of the danger which he posed to them and their community, though helpless to avert it.

Nora Atkins

Nora is the younger of the two Atkins cousins, just fifteen (her birthday was 14 July) and about to enter her last year at school, eagerly awaiting the time when she will leave school and be fully an adult. Although she is younger than Olivia, they are always grouped together by the adults and, indeed, by themselves, a relationship which they accept happily until the return of Stevens.

> Sœurs siamoises depuis notre enfance, jamais séparées, pleines de secrets non dits et partagés dans l'émerveillement de vivre. Il a suffi d'un seul regard posé sur nous deux ensemble, comme sur une seule personne, du fond de l'église, par un garçon insolent, pour que rien ne soit plus jamais comme avant entre nous. (121)

Suddenly the girls wish to be seen as individuals and are no longer prepared to be taken as a pair. They start to compete, wondering which of them is the more attractive to Stevens. Nora is longing to know which of them has the more beautiful breasts, and she is clearly jealous of Stevens's barely concealed preference for Olivia. When he praises the beauty of Olivia to Nora, she immediately lets him know that Olivia's beauty is marred by the presence of a small web on one of her feet, making her like a duck. Stevens wounds her pride by suggesting that she is jealous of her cousin, a remark which puts her to flight, furious and screaming abuse at him. Although he

---

[8] Bishop, *Anne Hébert*, p. 159, interprets Stevens's life as a succession of exiles, all of which increase the alienation and violence of Stevens.

despises and does not value women, he understands them well and has remarkable insight into the thoughts of both Nora and Olivia, which Nora in particular resents. She never forgives him for this insult, which rankles for the remaining days of her short life and leads directly to her death at his hands on the beach. Still hurt and angry, she refuses his arm and walks ahead while Stevens and Olivia hold hands on the moonlit beach. Stevens knows that she will never forgive his lack of interest in her, but the scene on the beach is peaceful enough until Nora breaks the peace by turning to hurl insults at him, her voice drowning the peaceful lapping of the waves. He begins to feel the storm gathering inside his head as she continues to cover him with insults questioning his masculinity and warning Olivia against him. When she repeats that he is not a real man and throws back her head to laugh hysterically, she exposes her throat which he means to stroke to calm her, but instead squeezes to silence her. Suddenly she has crumpled to her knees in front of him. In one sense Nora has caused her own death. She knew where to wound Stevens at his most sensitive point, by questioning his sexuality, and she does it in front of Olivia, which makes it worse. Her jealousy and her hurt pride give her the insight to attack Stevens at his most vulnerable, and his brutal, violent nature takes immediate revenge.

Ironically, Nora has the confidence to challenge and confront Stevens in the way she does because, alone of the main characters, she has had a happy childhood. Her parents seem to be happily married and fond of their children. Her father is clearly devoted to his daughters, while her mother offers love and affection. Nora is fond of her sisters and brothers, although that summer, as a typical adolescent, she is mainly concerned with herself, wondering about her attractiveness to boys and what the future will hold for her. She looks forward with confidence to a happy marriage in which she will give birth to lots of children, ten or twelve is her aim. Her fantasies focus on the young man who will become her husband. Her dreams include 'une espèce de roi' (**120**) who will make her the queen of oranges or of cotton; he will not be one of the local boys, but will come from far away. In another dream, as she lies listening to the skeins of geese migrating south for the winter she conjures up the image of a swan who will turn into a prince and abandon his flight to land on her roof one night, casting off his disguise as the spell is broken. The swan prince is replaced by a pirate captain, who will kidnap her from the beach and attach her to his prow as a figurehead to brave the elements as he sails the seas.[9] The pirate captain in turn

---

[9] Bishop, 'Énergie textuelle', p. 196, sees this as an example of the impossiblity of happiness in relations between men and women: 'Nora qui désire l'homme et qui rêve d'amour, semble deviner l'impossiblité de connaître une relation heureuse avec lui, et cela par la faute du sadisme inhérent au mâle dans cet univers romanesque.'

gives way to an American in a new Chevrolet or Buick, but she gives little time to this dream. Instead reality reasserts itself as she describes the arrival of Stevens, on foot, his boots covered in dust, his pack on his back, very different from the imaginary princes of her dreams, but nonetheless attractive and interesting.

Nora is well aware that she is attractive to boys and older men, and is fully enjoying the experience. She intends to have kissed them all by the end of the summer. Bob Allen and Patrick kiss her, but the former has bad breath (her mother says it is because he goes to the brothels), and she does not like the way Patrick nibbles her mouth and then asks if he kisses as well as Bob. She looks forward to being kissed by Stevens, when she will put her arms round his neck, but in the same moment remembers that he has insulted her and decides that she will resist. She is well aware of her effect on the American in the big car and, although she thinks that he is much too old and calls him a 'vieux salaud', she laughs as she does so and she knows that he does not take the insult too seriously. He is frightened off, however, by her uncle Nicolas, and Nora knows very well that Nicolas is very interested in her. She prays that her first lover will not be any of the local men, for all that she is willing to experiment with them. She is longing for 'fun' (**131**), but she wants someone who is new and different, not the boys she has known since childhood.

Nora is attracted to Stevens precisely because he does represent someone who is new and a little different. She was only ten or eleven when he left the village, and had been too young to play with him. She belonged with Olivia and Perceval and the younger children. He is therefore an unknown quantity, although he is also part of the extended family. He is undeniably attractive, and has a certain mystery about him which leads her to pursue him. She has already convinced herself that when he looked in at the church door and his gaze fell on her and Olivia, she was the one that he was really looking at. This one moment was enough to shatter the closeness between her and Olivia, as they both felt the attraction of this boy, who is, as Nora admits to herself, a 'voyou' (**122**). Nora is determined to prove that she is right and that Stevens is attracted to her. She remembers the autumn, when she went into the forest to bring food to the hunters and was warned by her mother to take care that they did not mistake her for a deer, of similar colouring. She was greeted with enthusiasm and Nicolas, no longer in clerical garb, flirted with her. Sidney offered her a drink, and her father, sensing what was happening, abruptly ordered her home. In summer she becomes the huntress and stalks Stevens through the wood. Although she knows what boys' bodies are like, she is still innocent enough not to understand fully the risks that she is running. The moment she steps on a branch, and Stevens turns to face her, the roles are reversed. Nora realises that she is the prey before him, although she wants to be his equal and to see his desire for her equal her desire for him. She is furious at her helplessness.

> C'est lui le chasseur et moi je tremble et je supplie quoique j'enrage d'être ainsi tremblante et suppliante en silence devant lui alors qu'il serait si facile de s'entendre comme deux personnes, égales entre elles, dans l'égalité de leur désir. (**127**)

Her dreams are shattered. She realises that there is no equality between them, and never can be, for Stevens is not interested in her:

> Son air méprisant. Ses yeux sans regard comme ceux des statues. Sa grande carcasse appuyée contre un sapin. Je crois qu'il a les mains dans les poches. Un instant de plus et il va se mettre à siffler. (**127**)

She is ready to offer herself to him, and he does not want her: 'L'affront en pleine face. Je ne lui pardonnerai jamais' (**127**). Her anger and resentment at his rejection have unexpected consequences. As she runs from him, through her mind flashes a nursery rhyme from the Catholics of Cap Sauvagine: 'Promenons-nous dans le bois pendant que le loup n'y est pas' (**128**). Walking on the beach calms her, but she is waiting for something to happen and it does: the wolf appears in the shape of her uncle Nicolas, in his clergyman's black. Nora knows that he realises she is angry and that this excites him. She lets him draw her into the boathouse, and he urges her to put aside her anger. As she realises her effect on him she becomes calmer. This male at least is subject to her sexual attractions. She sits on an overturned boat, allowing him to fondle her breast, bury his head in her lap, and feels herself responding as her nipples grow hard, allowing this to happen only because of Stevens's rejection of her (Randall, p. 70). The scene is rudely interrupted by Perceval pressing his face against the window and, as they hear him running across the beach to tell Irène, Nicolas leaps back from Nora:

> Il dit que je suis mauvaise. [...] Il dit que c'est par moi que le péché est entré à Griffin Creek. (**129**)

His guilt and frustration make him turn on her in anger.

The result, of course, is the first tragedy of Griffin Creek that summer. Irène commits suicide, but Nora is not unduly sympathetic:

> Ma tante Irène a commis son propre péché, au petit matin, dans la grange. Le péché de ma tante Irène est le plus grave de tous, celui qui ne pardonne pas, le même que celui de Judas qui est allé se pendre comme ma tante Irène. (**129-30**)

Although she weeps more than any of the other village women for Irène, Nora is well aware of the contrast between them.

> Ma tante Irène était faite pour le malheur et elle est morte. Paix à ses cendres grises.[10]
> Je suis faite pour vivre. Je crois bien que je ne mourrai jamais. (**131**)

Nora has all the confidence and arrogance of youth, of an attractive girl who has been loved by all around her. She is sorry for her dead aunt, but the implication is clear: colourless Irène had nothing to live for and is better off dead. Like Judas, Irène became an outcast who had no place in the community and no self-respect. The bitter irony is that Nora will soon be as dead as Irène, without in any way having fulfilled her promise or even had time to experience the life to which she is looking forward so eagerly. Her fate is every bit as tragic as the fate of Irène, but, unlike Irène, Nora is in large part responsible for her own fate, since it is her search for love and fulfilment which leads ultimately to her premature death.

Like her grandmother, Nora loves the sea, although she never learns to be a powerful swimmer, unlike Olivia, and despite all Patrick's efforts to teach her. Before dawn, their grandmother takes the two cousins to the beach so that, as the first pink glow touches the greyness of the sea, they can dive into 'l'âme nouvelle du soleil qui se déploie sur les vagues' (**113**) This is the time when Felicity is at her most approachable: 'douce et tendre, délivrée d'un enchantement'. (**113**) If the high tide is late and comes in broad daylight, Felicity refuses to bathe and her whole mood is different. Nora has other happy memories of the sea, crossing the bay at low tide in her Uncle John's cart, playing at making mud pies with Olivia and Perceval on the beach while their mothers knit in the distance. For her the sea is the source of her life: 'J'y suis née' (**116**). In a previous existence, for which her body still yearns, she was a sea creature able to stay in the water without breathing for long periods, something which she cannot recapture now even when Patrick coaches her in swimming. Sprung from earth and water like Adam, she was not made from Adam's rib but instead is unique, his equal and implicitly his rival.[11] She is the new Eve, aware of her own sexuality and her potential, and equally aware of the sexuality of the boys (which she attributes to their mothers) for whom she is waiting and with whom she is already tacitly communicating.

---

[10] There is a verbal echo here of the description of Irène by her husband when he talks about her 'regard de cendre' (**45**). Then she could force Nicolas to drop his gaze before her, but now, as Nora's words make clear, there is nothing left but ash.

[11] Bishop, 'Distance', p. 126: 'Le lecteur retiendra surtout, néanmoins, que Nora a élevé le désir féminin au statut d'égalité avec ce Dieu mâle qu'ont créé les hommes...'

Nora is still innocent and inexperienced, although she is not
ignorant. She is confident and happy, looking forward to life, to
leaving school, to sex, to marriage and child-bearing. She has no real
understanding of the dark passions in the men who surround her.
Although she childishly loses her temper with her uncle and with
Stevens and says that she hates them, she does not really understand
the risks she is running. She sees herself as a torch or a candle
lighting the summer darkness, but forgets that a candle can cause a
fire which will burn and destroy. Her uncle is obsessed with her
teenage beauty, to such an extent that his mother warns him to
control his behaviour. He ignores her warning, and when Nora, in
her rage against Stevens, is prepared to let Nicolas start to make love
to her, he cannot resist. The consequences are the death of Irène and
a lifetime of guilt for Nicolas. Nora knows the effect that she can
have on boys and is prepared to experiment, letting Bob Allen and
Patrick kiss her and expecting Stevens to take his turn before the end
of the summer. Stevens's lack of interest in her and preference for
Olivia are a challenge which she cannot resist, confident in her own
power and her knowledge of boys. At the last minute she discovers
that these are not as great as she had thought, and that Stevens can
reduce her from the pursuer to the suppliant, which she does not
enjoy at all and for which she will never forgive him. Thereafter she
is watching for an opportunity to take her revenge on Stevens for
rejecting and humiliating her. She does not understand him and his
desire to humiliate and humble women.[12] She feels that she is the
equal of men and that she can fight him on equal terms. She has
never suffered the unhappiness at home that Stevens and his brother
and his sisters have known, so that she has no fear of physical
violence from one of her relations. Her confidence in her own
powers and in her role as a woman destroy her, because she cannot
appreciate the violence and cruelty lurking behind the 'beau visage
dur' (**127**) of Stevens and, unlike Olivia, she has no fear of him. She
does not hear the ancestral voices which warn Olivia against Stevens.
She is not so modest and reserved as her cousin. Her horrible death
is the result of the very qualities which make her so fearless and
attractive, of her sheltered and happy upbringing, which gave her the
confidence to face men as equals and denied her the knowledge of
their violent passions. In her own way Nora is, quite unconsciously,
a destructive force partly responsible for the deaths of Irène and
Olivia as well as her own death. Her sex appeal, her beauty, her
courage, her innocence all contribute to the disaster.

---

[12] Bishop, 'Distance', p. 120: 'Stevens a une vision fort sexiste de Nora, la méprisant à cause
du désir qu'elle éprouve pour lui.'

Olivia Atkins

Her cousin Olivia, whose beauty provokes Nora's jealousy, is a very different girl. She is two years older than Nora, although they are so often treated as twin sisters and even regard themselves in that light until the return of Stevens. Her home life is not as happy as Nora's, for her mother is dead, and her father and two elder brothers, for whom she keeps house, watch over her incessantly. Little stress is put on the drudgery of life for the women of Griffin Creek, although it is clear that the pastor tyrannises the twins, who slave at keeping his house tidy and seeing to his every whim. This could be dismissed as an exception, however, as an aged widower and his two simple-minded servants hardly constitues a normal household, but the brief references to Olivia's life at home also show how hard the women had to work. Stevens first catches Olivia while she is ironing, and his presence so distracts her that she burns the sleeve of one of the shirts. The next time he visits her, she is struggling to hang out the washing in a violent wind which whips the heavy sheets away from her. Her brothers are drinking beer on the veranda when Stevens comes up behind her, but none of the men lift a finger to help her although she is obviously having problems with the buffeting and twisting sheets. The noise of the sheets blowing in the wind and wrapping themselves round her anticipates the night of the murder. The flapping of her skirts, as Stevens rapes her, reminds him of the flapping of the sheets which she was hanging out.

The scene which says most about the harshness of life for the women is one recalled by Olivia. She thinks about her dead mother, and remembers how only two days before her death she was struggling to bring in the potato harvest from the prematurely hard, frosty ground. Young as she was, Olivia knew that her mother was far from well and seemed far too tired. When her mother said that she could rest only when the job was done, Olivia did what she could to help so that her mother would be able to rest all the sooner. Again there is no suggestion that the men might help with what was, after all, a physically demanding task. The kitchen garden was the domain of the women, and the men would not interfere.

Olivia's efforts are, of course, in vain, as her mother dies, with her last breath making the men promise to watch over Olivia, and bidding Olivia to be obedient and a good housekeeper. From that moment Olivia is a prisoner in her own house, guarded by her brothers, with whom she cannot communicate because of their masculine contempt for girls. Stevens, too, abandons her to join with her brothers. There are other suggestions that the home life of Olivia is not as happy as that of Nora. Her mother is quieter and more

subdued than Nora's lively mother, who knows everything that goes
on in the village without even having to try to find it out. Olivia
wonders why her mother is always so sad, as if she were looking at
terrible, invisible things which no one else can see. Olivia suspects
that she is saddened by the noise made by her husband in their
wooden house, or by the noisy swearing of her brothers as they try
to assert their masculinity. Olivia sees blood on her mother's sheets
and has no idea where it comes from or who has caused it. The little
girl unconsciously feels a sense of feminine solidarity with her
mother, and wants to comfort and reassure her, to take her away
somewhere magical like the depths of the sea, where she can recover
her lost youth, by implication destroyed by Olivia's father and
brothers.

> Au fond des océans peut-être, là où il y a des palais de coquillages, des
> fleurs étranges, des poissons multicolores, des rues où l'on respire l'eau
> calmement comme l'air. Nous vivrons ensemble sans bruit et sans
> effort. (**208**)

Already as a small child, Olivia, anticipating her destiny, sees the sea
as a place of refuge and security for women. Later after the death of
her mother she will sit by the sea, watching the tide come in and
trying to understand the mystery of life and of the death of her
mother. Always, just at the moment when she is about to understand
everything and to see in the water the face of the dead woman, the
spell is broken by the shouts of her brothers. She has to climb back
up the cliff into her identity, and take up her life again.

Olivia is very much aware of this feeling of feminine solidarity.
A recurrent theme in the section of the book narrated by her is that
she can hear the voices of her female ancestors carried on the wind
and coming from the sea, warning her against Stevens, to whom she
is strongly attracted. When her ghost returns to the village, brought
in by the high tide, it is Stevens for whom she is searching, although
she does not immediately name him. Instead she glides through
houses like Maureen's which have been abandoned, or into the
dreams of her uncle, but all to no purpose.

> J'ai beau siffler dans le trou des serrures, me glisser sous les lits sans
> couvertures ni matelas, souffler les poussières fines, faire bouffer le
> volant de cretonne fanée du cosy-corner dans le petit salon de ma
> cousine Maureen, me faufiler toute mouillée dans les songes de mon
> oncle Nicolas, emmêler les tresses blondes des petites servantes de mon
> oncle Nicolas; celui que je cherche n'est plus ici. (**199-200**)

She is looking for her murderer, as her opening remark makes
clear: 'Il y a certainement quelqu'un qui m'a tuée. Puis s'en est allé.

Sur la pointe des pieds' (**199**).[13] From this moment the reader is involved, and the search is on for the murderer (Ouellette-Michalska, p. 32). At the end of Olivia's visit to the dying village, she experiences again those dreadful last moments on the beach.

> Que je lève seulement la tête et je verrai son visage, la dureté de ses os ruisselants de lune. Ses lèvres se retroussent sur ses dents en un sourire étrange. Mon Dieu vais-je mourir à nouveau? (**224**)

The memory of it drives her to flight, her quest unresolved, back to the security of the ocean, away from the fury of the night of 31 August 1936.

Unlike Nora, who rests at peace in the graveyard of the village, Olivia's body was never discovered, and she is now part of the sea and the air.

> Pur esprit d'eau ayant été dépouillé de mon corps sur des bancs de sable et des paquets de sel, mille poissons aveugles ont rongé mes os. (**207**)

This is her environment, for she has always felt at home in the sea, allowed to share it with her grandmother and taught to swim so well by her brother, that Stevens briefly mistakes her for him, Patrick, the swimming instructor (**96**). When the memories get too oppressive for her ghost, her first thought is to flee and to rejoin the wind which will bear her away from the dangers of Griffin Creek.

> Fuir. Rejoindre la marée qui se retire jusqu'au plus haut point de l'épaisseur des eaux. Le grand large. Son souffle rude. Filer sur la ligne d'horizon. Épouser le vent, glisser sur les pentes lisses du vent, planer comme un goéland invisible. (**207**)

Instead she lingers, remembering that she was thrown still alive into the moonlit sea, and her thoughts return to Stevens as a little boy.

Olivia is closer to Stevens than Nora can ever be. Nora wanted him for herself to prove she was irresistible; Olivia had been close to him as a child. She remembers a beach scene when she was three or four making sand pies, suddenly sensing that he is there behind her and, with a sideways glance, taking in everything about him:

> lumineux et doré, nimbé de lumière pâle, la tête à moitié perdue dans le ciel et le vent, comme un soleil pâle échevelé... (**205**)

'Nimbé de lumière' is an echo of the description of Stevens as 'inondé de lumière' (**121**) when he looked into the church while

---

[13] This is a quotation from Anne Hébert's *Les Songes en équilibre,* poèmes (Montréal: Éditions de l'Arbre, 1942).

Nicolas was taking a service, and with one glance severed the closeness of the Atkins cousins. She knows already that he admires her, as they hold hands and shout in triumph at her handiwork, but the scene is broken by one of the mothers calling to them, and Stevens runs away, ignoring his father who is whistling from the top of the cliff as if he were calling his dog. Olivia screams a warning, but in a cloud of pebbles and sand Stevens's father comes down the cliff, captures his son, and shakes him fiercely. Already, at the age of seven, Stevens sets his will against the will of the adult world and is in conflict with his father.

Despite her wish to escape from this memory, Olivia remembers the feel of his fingers against her cheek as they shouted with joy like Perceval, shouts which quickly turned to fear when John Brown seized hold of his son. She remembers too the one occasion when she was allowed to join in the boys' games and how, at the end before he ran off with the other boys, Stevens came over. In the summer heat she could smell his masculinity and knew that he too was experiencing her 'senteur de fille', an experience which summed up for her all the joy of being in Griffin Creek. The memory makes the ghost long to resume her human form, to walk on the water back to Griffin Creek, but instead she slides back into the house, carried along by the gusts of wind to experience the time when she was ironing, surrounded by the voices of her female ancestors, as, like them, she carried out the tasks of women: 'La longue lignée des gestes de femme à Griffin Creek pour la lier à jamais' **(215)**. When Stevens appears she recognises him at once, even after five years of absence which have turned him into a man. She does not admit that she knows him, while the voices in the wind beg her to pretend ignorance and to go on ironing as if nothing had happened.[14]

> Je les entends qui disent; Ne lève pas la tête de ton repassage, tant que ce mauvais garçon sera là dans la porte. **(215)**

Stevens is temptation:

> Il est comme l'arbre planté au milieu du paradis terrestre. La science du bien et du mal n'a pas de secret pour lui. Si seulement je voulais bien j'apprendrais tout de lui, d'un seul coup, la vie, la mort, tout. **(216)**

Love with Stevens would make her a woman like her ancestors and put her on a footing of equality with them. Throughout the summer she wrestles with the inner voices warning her against Stevens and

---

[14] Randall, p. 67, shows the limitations of female power: 'l'évidence textuelle réduit ce féminisme inconscient à peu de chose: aux voix des femmes-ancêtres soufflant dans le vent mais impuissantes à sauver Olivia et Nora du sort que leur destine, semble-t-il, leur propre désir.'

the strength of her desire for him (Bishop, 'Distance', p. 120). She is determined that he must not know how she feels.

> Surtout qu'il ne s'aperçoive de rien. S'il me voyait rougir devant lui, à cause de lui qui me tourmente, une fois, une fois seulement et je mourrais de honte. (**217**)

The memories are too painful for the ghost, and Olivia wants to regain the safety of the high seas, where the sound of ancestral voices mingles with the cries of the whales. One last memory, however, is the barn dance where she touches Stevens but carefully keeps her eyes lowered, as advised by her voices. She is cut to the quick when she hears Nora laughing as she dances with Stevens. Olivia does not know that Nora is furious with Stevens and pretending to be unaware of him.

As the summer wears on, Olivia's frustrated desire occupies the whole of her mind. She is longing to see Stevens, to be touched by him, before he leaves again for Florida. When he staggers drunkenly into the house of Nora's parents to beg Olivia and Nora to go with him to experience the fury of the storm, Olivia is ready to succumb. If Stevens had spoken to her alone she would have gone with him, staggering and stinking of alcohol as he was. The sharp voice of her Aunt Alice intervenes, the voice of her female relations, to say that not even a dog should be out in such weather. One more call and she would have gone, so great is her longing for Stevens, but he is incapable of speaking and collapses over the table with his head on his arms. The growing rift between the two cousins is made more apparent that night, when Olivia refuses to share the bed of Nora any longer. Instead, with her need to be alone, she lies awake at the foot of Nora's bed, listening to the untroubled breathing of Nora and her little sisters, while she hears her name being called and ten times gets up to go to the window and try to see out through the pouring rain.

> Le désir d'une fille qui appelle dans une chambre fermée, alors que ses mère et grand-mères grondent tout alentour de la maison, affirment que ce garçon est mauvais, soûl comme une bourrique, et qu'il ne faut pas l'écouter, sous peine de se perdre avec lui. (**222-3**)

Olivia remains, just, in control of her emotions, although well aware of the struggle that is raging inside her.

Her memory leaps from one storm to the next, trying to avoid the period in between. As they had been linked in life, the cousins are joined as they lie in death at the bottom of the bay, until the October gales disturb them. Then Nora is washed ashore to be recognised and buried, while Olivia is swept out to sea by the current, her body dissolved by the salt so that only her soul, as infinitesimal as a tear, is left in the vastness of the ocean. Her ghost cannot endure the memory of the night of 31 August. She cannot face the recollection of the smile of Stevens that night or the thought of a second death.

> Je n'ai que juste le temps de me couvrir d'ombre comme un poulpe dans son encre, m'échapper sur la mer avant que ne revienne, dans toute sa furie, la soirée du 31 août 1936. (**225**)

Olivia is now at the mercy of the wind and tide, but she knows that really it is her unsatisfied desire that brings her ghost back to Griffin Creek (Backès, p. 55). In spite of the urgings of her mother and grandmothers, she comes back to haunt Griffin Creek, to relive the summer of 1936, the last one she lived and the first one she truly experienced.

> Non, non ce n'est pas moi, c'est le désir qui me tire et m'amène, chaque jour, sur la grève. J'en demande pardon aux grandes femmes liquides, mes mère et grand-mères. Un certain été, un certain visage ruisselant de lune se trouvent à Griffin Creek. Non pas dans le présent des maisons délabrées et désertes, mais dans l'éternité sauvage de la terre. Je hante Griffin Creek afin que renaisse l'été 1936. (**221**)

Olivia, like her uncle, feels guilt over the events of that summer. She blames herself for her failure to control her feelings for Stevens. As children they had always been close, and as a young man and woman they are both aware of an overwhelming sexual attraction. Olivia is not like Nora, wanting to add Stevens to her list of conquests. Her fondness for the boy cousin who showed her a little more consideration and admiration than the other boys is maturing into love and longing for an attractive young man, despite the sinister reputation which surrounds him. Everything warns her that he is dangerous, and yet she can barely resist him. She knows that he is interested in her but just as she tantalises him by concealing her feelings, so he keeps her guessing as to whether he prefers her to Nora. Olivia feels the same jealousy as Nora driving a wedge between them, but she lacks Nora's happy confidence and her feeling of equality with men. Olivia comes from a household where the men oppressed the women at the same time as they guarded them. There is little tenderness or gratitude to give Olivia a sense of her own value. Her mother, who would in any case have been a frail support with her ill-health and her silence, is dead, and the voices of Olivia's mother and grandmothers are forever warning her against men, and in particular Stevens. Olivia is not so confident of her beauty as Nora, although to Stevens she is the more beautiful, for which Nora will never forgive him. She is more timid and less provocative, not realising that these very traits make her all the more alluring to

Stevens. She cannot guess at the savagery of his feelings against all women, and her especially:

> Une telle excitation dans tout mon corps, une rage inexplicable. Il y a trop de femmes dans ce village, trop de femmes en chaleur [...]. Olivia est plus coriace, résistante dans sa peur de moi... (**80**)

Her beauty, her modesty, and the fact that she is almost unattainable drive him on to pursue her, while he can reject easily Nora when she offers herself to him. Even when he is ready to leave for Florida, which is where he longs to be, Stevens cannot resist one last time with Olivia, intercepting her and Nora as they leave Maureen's house. The girls feel safe together and are willing to walk on the moonlit beach with him, where the tragedy is brought about by Nora's jealousy and fury unleashing the evil lurking within Stevens, an evil of which they were all half-consciously aware. With Nora dead, Olivia cannot be allowed to live. Once Stevens has tackled her to the ground, she is vulnerable to his lust, and with his greater strength he can rape her in an obscene parody of her desire to wrestle with him as she had wrestled with him when he surprised her after her bathe.

> Un jour, mon amour, nous nous battrons tous les deux sur la grève, dans la lumière de la lune qui enchante et rend fou. Sans grâce ni merci. Jusqu'à ce que l'un de nous touche le sable des deux épaules, le temps de compter une minute. (**202**)

The scene of the night of 31 August matches her fantasy precisely, but even as she fantasised, she sensed that she was in danger. She is aware of the danger of the moon and the moonlight and their effect on Stevens, whose appearance now alters so much:

> Cet homme est mauvais. Il ne désire rien tant que de réveiller la plus profonde épouvante en moi pour s'en repaître comme d'une merveille. (**202**)

In fact Stevens wants to defile her, to treat her as a tart, to punish her for seeming so pure and inviolable:

> L'injurier en paix. L'appeler salope. La démasquer, elle, la fille trop belle et trop sage. À tant faire l'ange on... Lui faire avouer qu'elle est velue, sous sa culotte, comme une bête. Le défaut caché de sa belle personne solennelle, cette touffe noire et humide entre ses cuisses là où je fornique comme chez les guidounes... (**248**)

Olivia is the tragic victim of the passions of others. Her feeling of guilt is misplaced as she has nothing with which to reproach herself in either the death of her mother or her own behaviour. Her very virtues cause her death, but unburied and unsatisfied, her ghost cannot leave the scene where for one last summer she was alive and experiencing love. Instead she is washed in and out by the tide, aware that the sea is where she now belongs and is safe. There is nothing left for her in Griffin Creek, which now belongs to the last remnants of the bygone age of her youth. Her place is with the spirits of her ancestors on the open sea, the eternal symbol of femininity.

> Légère comme une bulle, écume de mer salée, plus rapide que la pensée, plus agile que le songe...Pareille à quelque oiseau de mer, mollement balancée entre deux vagues, je regarde l'étendue de l'eau, à perte de vue, se gonfler, se distendre comme le ventre d'une femme sous la poussée de son fruit. (**204**)

Conclusion

Griffin Creek in the summer of 1936 is a place where nothing seems to happen and nothing changes very much, until the arrival of Stevens disturbs the surface tranquillity. The tranquillity is only superficial, because the passions and the memories which the arrival of Stevens brings into the open are already there: the cruelty of John Brown, the coldness of Bea Brown, the contempt of Felicity Jones for Peter, her husband, the repressed sexuality of her son Nicolas and the fight between father and son which drove Stevens out of the village five years before, to name but a few. Five years of bumming around the States have turned Stevens into a hard, uncaring young man, very attractive to women but filled with hatred for them. The only woman spared this contempt is his grandmother, Felicity, but he can harden his soul against her too. His initial wish to seek her absolution on his return to the village is quickly dismissed. Stevens has no wish to be completely reintegrated into the village. He regards himself as a bird of passage, pausing for the summer to make some money before he returns to Florida and Old Mic. Griffin Creek has formed and shaped him, however, and he is the most extreme example of the masculine dominance and cruelty which make the women of Griffin Creek suffer and die.

The war between men and women seems to affect every family in Griffin Creek except the family of Ben and Alice Atkins. Whereas Olivia is aware of the violence of men, exemplified by the noisy swearing of her brothers and their swift rejection of their mother's affection as they become adolescents, Nora has no reason to fear them. Her father and her brother are kind to her, and obviously fond of her. Olivia is aware that, after the death of her mother, she becomes the slave of her menfolk, a possession which they guard fiercely against possible thieves or interlopers. Her mother led a crushed, near-silent existence, prematurely aged, possibly the victim of wife-beating, and there is nothing in her life or her afterlife to give Olivia confidence in men. Olivia fears men, whereas Nora challenges them. The tragedy is that neither attitude can protect them against the violence of men. The physically stronger sex can always do the greater damage eventually, but Hébert makes clear that the men are taking revenge for the damage done to them by women. The infidelities of Peter Jones alienate his wife Felicity so much that she has no love for her son Nicolas, who grows up desperate for her love and approval, desperate too to have childen who will replace his nieces in the affections of their grandmother. The sterility of his unattractive wife Irène means that both his ambitions are frustrated, and he is painfully aware that he is living a lie. He is a man of God,

the leader of his community, preaching hellfire and damnation to his
congregation in his beautiful voice which he has so carefully
cultivated. He knows that this is a sham. He is his father's son,
driven, as his mother says, by demons, who longs for sexual
satisfaction and whose frustration makes him a voyeur prepared to
commit incest with his niece. Even though he knows it is wrong, he
cannot resist the temptation when it is offered to him, although
afterwards he is filled with guilt and self-loathing which he
immediately diverts to his niece. He has already shown, when he
slapped her face for flirting with the American, that he is ready to
use violence on her, and he knows that in the depths of his soul he is
not different from the other men of Griffin Creek, who kill animals
and violate their wives. He has to live for the rest of his life with this
knowledge and with his guilt and shame for causing the death of
Irène, but his cruelty and contempt for women are not lessened by
this knowledge. He continues to treat his inoffensive servants, the
twins Pam and Pat, cousins of Nora and Olivia and their harmless
and unattractive doubles, with cruelty and contempt.

> Sans jamais avoir été femmes, les voici qui subissent leur retour d'âge,
> avec le même air étonné que leurs premières règles. Pas une once de
> graisse, ni seins, ni hanches, fins squelettes d'oiseaux. (**17**)

He finds pleasure in humiliating and dominating them, although he
stops well short of causing them physical pain. In this respect he
differs from Stevens.

Stevens takes a sadistic pleasure in defiling women. He is
permanently damaged by the lack of affection of his mother and the
harshness of his father. Cruel and unloving parents have killed his
capacity for affection where women are concerned. He can feel
affection for his brother Perceval, and perhaps for old Mic, and
when he was younger he clearly felt affection for Olivia. On his
return to the village he finds her a woman and sexually attractive,
but he cannot seduce her because he is inhibited by the conventions
of the village that unmarried girls of a respectable family are
untouchable, and thwarted by the care with which she is protected.
He does not intend marriage, as he prefers his freedom in Florida
(where Olivia would willingly follow him), and has to seek sexual
release with the prostitutes in the nearby town or, when he can force
himself to do it, with Maureen. Both gestures are expressions of his
contempt for women and his need for revenge on them. He is never
able to treat women in any other way. During the war he rapes and
kills, echoing the events of the night of 31 August, when his
masculinity was questioned and a woman, although Nora was hardly
that yet, dared to challenge him. Stevens had no answer to Nora's

contempt and hatred except an act of violence that will prove his masculinity. Having once resorted to violence to silence Nora, he then had to continue to use it to silence Olivia, who had been the unwilling witness. All his pent-up resentment and hatred are poured into the rape and then the murder of his cousin.[1] Ever since his return he has been angered by the self-control of Olivia, who has taken pains to keep him at arm's length. Stevens despises women, but he does not like women who resist him. If, like Maureen or Nora, they offer themselves to him, then he can be indifferent to them, but Olivia's indifference to him is a challenge to his masculine authority. In the end he asserts it violently, and Olivia dies, the latest in a line of female victims in Griffin Creek who have suffered at the hands of men who dominate society and cannot, in the last resort, even punish Stevens for his crime (Slott, 'Submersion', p. 160; Bishop, *Anne Hébert*, p. 175).

Hébert does not absolve her female characters, however, from their share of the responsibility.[2] The boys are offered unattractive role models in the shape of fathers such as Peter Jones and John Brown, who are cruel or unfaithful and alienate their wives, but Felicity Jones and Bea Brown do nothing to compensate for the failures of their husbands. Felicity rigorously excludes her son from any part of her private world, and then feeds his jealousy by sharing it with her granddaughters. Bea is cold and unloving even before her children are born. She accepts totally her husband's attitude to his children, as Stevens remembers from his childhood:

> j'entends la grande ombre double qui chuchote derrière la mince cloison. Il est question d'enfants qui ne doivent pas naître et d'enfants déjà nés qu'il faut perdre en forêt, avant qu'ils ne soient trop grands. (85)

This brutal and uncaring home alienated the boy from all normal human affection, so that he grows up damaged emotionally and ready to seek revenge on those who made him suffer. He takes his revenge on the next generation of girls, who also provokes him by tempting or resisting him. Temporarily he is removed from society while awaiting trial. Then, after his acquittal, he is soon removed from Canada by the 1939-1945 war, where he takes part in yet more dreadful violence, much of it against women, and his experiences leave him a permanent invalid in hospital. Here he loses part of his masculine identity, learning to weep and to knit. After his escape

---

[1] Hillenaar, p. 8: 'Même le meurtre que commet Stevens dans *Les Fous de Bassan* ne s'explique pas sans la conduite de tous ces parents qui sont intervenus ou interviennent dans la vie du jeune assassin aussi bien que dans celle des deux victimes.'

[2] Randall, pp. 67-8: 'la froideur maternelle de Bea et de Félicité, la vengeance sexuelle, la jalousie et la provocation exercées par Nora ne semblent guère correspondre ni à la vertu ni à la moralité.'

from hospital he is isolated in his room, sleeping by day and waking by night to write his account of 1936 to old Mic, the only one in whom he can confide.

Stevens, however, is only the worst of the sinners of Griffin Creek. In his old age, Nicolas Jones realises that Griffin Creek has always been full of evil:

> Non, ce n'est pas Stevens qui a manqué le premier, quoiqu'il soit le pire de nous tous, le dépositaire de toute la malfaisance secrète de Griffin Creek, amassée au cœur des hommes et des femmes depuis deux siècles. (**27**)

In part this stems from their pride, seeing themselves as a people chosen by God, a people who have tamed their country:

> Je murmure les mots qu'ils attendent de moi. Cette louange, cette exaltation d'eux-mêmes et de leur vocation de peuple élu, dans un pays sauvage, face à la mer, dos à la montagne. (**31**)

Nicolas Jones knows that sin cannot be rooted out easily, even with the example of Christ before us:

> *Nous savons en effet que le vieil homme en nous a été crucifié afin que soit aboli le corps du péché, pour que nous ne soyons plus asservis au péché.*
> Il n'est plus facile de chasser l'homme ancien, le voici qui persiste, s'incruste en moi comme une tique, entre chair et cuir. (**39**)

He knows that he is part of the community of sinners, like the other men of Griffin Creek. Despite his vocation and his sense of being called by God, in his innermost soul he is their brother in sin and, in his old age, he can look on the misfortune of the community:

> Appelé par Dieu, tiré du limon de Griffin Creek, par Dieu, pour accomplir l'image parfaite de l'agneau à l'intérieur de mon âme, au creux le plus secret de mes os, voici que je n'en finis pas de retourner à la terre originelle et d'être l'un d'eux, parmi eux, mes frères sauvages et durs. Le malheur de Griffin Creek est devant moi, entre cap Sec et cap Sauvagine. (**40**)

Griffin Creek is doomed, and the pastor has to watch its slow death, knowing that he will not discover the whole truth until the Day of Judgement, when he will finally be absolved of his sins. In his dreams he sees Perceval as the angel of the Apocalypse, the head of a cherub on the body of a man, blowing the trumpet for the Day of Judgement. Nicolas knows that Perceval saw the truth, although he never revealed what he knew. His apocalyptic vision puts Perceval firmly among the innocent, unlike almost everyone else.

The theme of *Les Fous de Bassan* is sexual desire as part of the
unending conflict between men and women.[3] In Hébert's vision, men
are predators and women are their prey and their victims.[4] Any
woman rash enough to challenge the superiority of the male is in
danger, whether her challenge takes the form of a search for
equality, as in the case of Nora, or evasions and withdrawal, as in the
case of Olivia. Even immediate surrender, as in the case of Maureen,
is not without its risks; she is humiliated and broken by her
experiences of 1936, while her cousins are destroyed. No one
emerges unscathed from that summer, male or female, and there is
no way of resolving the conflict which destroys the community. The
men tolerate no challenge to their authority, and no change in the
traditional role of women.[5] The happy upbringing of Nora, which
gives her the confidence and the assurance to seek to confront
Stevens on equal terms, is shown to be just as likely to lead to
destruction as the cocooned and oppressive family life led by Olivia.

Anne Hébert has a deeply pessimistic view of the relations
between men and women. In *Les Fous de Bassan* they can never meet
on equal terms, and hardly ever with affection or love. The cruelty,
the violence and the arrogance of the men alienate the women, who
respond with coldness and indifference, withdrawing their love from
their children, in particular their sons, who will in turn become
violent, arrogant men in the next generation. Although women are
not absolved entirely from the responsibility for this bitter conflict,
they are the eternal losers, suffering at the hands of men whether in
peace or war.[6] For consolation they have to turn to the sea, the

[3] Sirois, p. 182: 'L'innocence et le bonheur édéniques ne sont que relatifs dans son récit, le fruit alléchant est devenu celui du sexe, contre lequel mettent les adolescentes en garde toutes les mères et grandmères de Griffin Creek, parce que sa manducation conduit à la domination de l'homme sur la femme. L'arbre de la connaissance du bien et du mal, le tentateur, le serpent avec toutes ses connotations sexuelles, sont identifiés à l'homme.'

[4] Bishop, 'Énergie', p. 188: 'Nul exemple, dans ce roman, d'un désir masculin non-destructeur; même la femme du pasteur est acculée au suicide par la faute du désir adultère et incestueux de son mari pour ses jeunes nièces.'

[5] Slott, 'Submersion', p. 298: 'Nora and Olivia Atkins begin to exercise their own voices, to reclaim the power of self-expression and to speak freely of their desire. Their success is an ironic one, for Nora is murdered because of the threat that her powerful voice poses to the dominant male culture, and Olivia must be murdered before she can even discover her true voice.' This is true, but Slott goes on to argue that nonetheless the book sees a 'resurgence of female energy and power', and this does not seem to be supported by a close reading of the text as Marilyn Randall has already suggested. Bishop (*Anne Hébert*, p. 201) argues that in spite of Randall's criticisms, the book is nonetheless a feminist book: 'il reste que *Les Fous de Bassan* constitue un roman féministe, c'est-à-dire un roman dont la dimension conative (Jakobson) manifeste l'intention de dénoncer la violence et les injustices que subissent les femmes dans une certaine société.' However, he then refers to contradictory aspects of the novel which would seem to undermine his argument.

[6] Bishop, *Anne Hébert*, p. 224: 'Tout comme *Les Fous de Bassan* se termine par l'expression, via le post-scriptum final de Stevens Brown, de la révolte de l'auteure contre un système politico-juridico-policier qui laisse impunis le viol et le meurtre...'. Rea., p. 180: 'In her text, Hébert is talking about the violence done to children by parents, the violence done to women by men, the violence done to humanity by war.'

symbol of the womb and the everlasting nature of woman. Their only refuge and release are in death (Senécal, p. 151). The title, with its twofold meaning, refers not only to the birds crying wildly and plunging violently into the sea to violate it, but to the men who resemble them in their violence and in their violation of the women, who identify with the sea.[7] Madness, death and unhappiness are the lot of even the chosen people, whose sins of lust and pride reach their apogee in the summer of 1936.[8]

---

[7] Randall, p. 71: 'Il n'y aurait aucun doute que le pouvoir des femmes se manifeste à travers leur relation à la mer et au vent, dont la puissance, liée aux origines créatrices du monde, envahit la vie entière de Griffin Creek.'

[8] Senécal, p. 154: 'The moral and theological climate of *In the Shadow of the Wind* underscores that the collective dementia that grips Griffin Creek one dark summer is the fulfillment of an inexorable curse, not the determinism of history or the hubris of man.'

Bibliography

Anne Hébert's relevant works having been mentioned in the text, the bibliography contains only books and articles pertaining to *Les Fous de Bassan* which have influenced my interpretation. There is a vast secondary literature on Hébert, as can be seen in the bibliography to Neil Bishop's *Anne Hébert, son œuvre, leurs exils,* which the author modestly says is not complete. It is, however, the most up-to-date at the moment of writing.

Translation

> *In the Shadow of the Wind,* translator Sheila Fischman. Toronto: Stoddart, 1983.

Film Adaptation

> *Les Fous de Bassan* (1987), directed by Yves Simoneau, starring Steve Banner, Charlotte Valandrey, Laure Marsac and Bernard-Pierre Donnadieu.

Interviews

> With Jean Royer, *Le Devoir* (11 décembre 1982), p. 21.
>
> 'Lointaine et proche Anne Hébert', with Brigitte Morissette *Châtelaine* (février 1983), pp. 53-4.

Critical Works

Backès, Jean-Louis   'Le Retour des morts dans l'œuvre d'Anne Hébert', *L'Esprit créateur*, XXIII, 3 (Fall 1983), 48-57.

Bishop, Neil B.   'Distance, point de vue, voix et idéologie dans *Les Fous de Bassan* d'Anne Hébert', *Voix et Images,* IX, 2, (hiver 1984), 113-29.

Bishop, Neil B.

'Énergie textuelle et production de sens: images de l'énergie dans *Les Fous de Bassan* d'Anne Hébert', *University of Toronto Quarterly,* LIV, 2 (hiver 1984-1985), 178-99.

——————

Anne Hébert, son œuvre, leurs exils. Presses Universitaires de Bordeaux, 1993.

Cauchon, Paul

'Simoneau et *Les Fous de Bassan:* «On a fait un contre les vagues...»', *Le Devoir,* 28 juillet 1986, pp. C-1 et C-4.

Émond, Maurice

La Femme à la fenêtre. Presses de l'Université de Laval, 'Vie des Lettres Québécoises, 22', 1984.

——————

'Un nouveau roman d'Anne Hébert', *Québec français,* 48 (décembre 1982), 13.

Ewing, Ronald

'Griffin Creek: The English World of Anne Hébert', *Canadian Literature,* 105 (Summer 1985), 100-110.

Francoli, Yvette

'Griffin Creek: refuge des *Fous de Bassan* et des bessons fous', *Études littéraires,* XVII, 1 (avril 1984), 131-42.

Gasquy-Resch, Yannick

Littérature du Québec (Vanves: E.D.I.C.E.F. / A.U.P.E.L.F., 1994), pp. 132-6.

Gould, Karen

'Absence and Meaning in Anne Hébert's *Les Fous de Bassan*', *French Review,* LIX, 6, (May 1986), 921-30.

Hillenaar, Henk

'Anne Hébert et le "roman familial" de Freud', in *Le Roman québécois depuis 1960,* ed. Louise Milot et Jaap Lintvelt (Presses de l'Université de Laval, 1992), pp. 1-15.

Lamy, Suzanne

'Le Roman de l'irresponsabilité', *Spirale,* 29 (novembre 1982), 3; 2.

Marcotte, Gilles

'*Les Fous de Bassan:* le grand roman de la rentrée', *L'Actualité,* VII, 10 (1982), 129.

Mélançon, Robert

'Ce qui est sans nom ni date', *Liberté,* XXV, 145 (février 1983), 89-93.

Merler, Grazia

'*Les Fous de Bassan* d'Anne Hébert devant la critique', *Œuvres et Critiques*, XIV, 1 (1989), 39-44.

Mésavage, Ruth

'L'Herméneutique de l'écriture: *Les Fous de Bassan* d'Anne Hébert', *Québec Studies*, 5 (1987), 111-24.

Noble, Peter

'The Thirties in Anne Hébert and Antonine Maillet', *London Journal of Canadian Studies*, IX (forthcoming).

Ouellette-Michalska, Madeleine

'Anne Hébert. L'Attrait du double', *Le Devoir*, 11 septembre 1982, pp. 17; 32.

Paterson, Janet M.

'L'Envolée de l'écriture: *Les Fous de Bassan* d'Anne Hébert', *Voix et Images*, IX, 3 (printemps 1984), 143-51.

——————

Anne Hébert: architexture romanesque. Éditions de l'Université d'Ottawa, 1985.

——————

'Anne Hébert: une poétique d'anaphore', in *Le Roman contemporain au Québec (1960-1985)*, ed. François Gallays, Sylvain Simard et Robert Vigneault (Montréal: Fides, 'Archives des Lettres Canadiennes, VIII', 1992), pp. 287-302.

Poulin, Gabrielle

'L'Écriture enchantée: *Les Fous de Bassan* d'Anne Hébert', *Lettres Québécoises*, 28 (hiver 1982-1983), 15-18.

Randall, Marilyn

'Les Énigmes des *Fous de Bassan:* féminisme, narration et clôture', *Voix et Images*, 43 (automne 1989), 66-82.

Rea, Annabelle

'The Climate of Viol / Violence and Madness in Anne Hébert's *Les Fous de Bassan*', *Québec Studies*, 4 (1986), 170-83.

Roy, Lucille

Entre la lumière et l'ombre. L'Univers poétique d'Anne Hébert. Sherbrooke (Québec): Éditions Naaman, coll. 'Thèses ou recherches, 17', 1984.

Senécal, André J.

'*Les Fous de Bassan:* an Eschatology', *Québec Studies*, 7 (1988), 150-60.

Sirois, Antoine   'Bible, mythes et *Fous de Bassan* d'Anne
                         Hébert', *Canadian Literature,* 104 (Spring
                         1985), 178-82.

Slott, Kathryn   'Submersion and Resurgence of the Female
                         Other in Anne Hébert's *Les Fous de Bassan'*,
                         Québec Studies, 4 (1986), 158-69.

—————————   'Repression, Obsession and Re-emergence in
                         Hébert's *Les Fous de Bassan'*, *American
                         Review of Canadian Studies,* XVII, 3 (1987),
                         297-307.

—————————   'From Agent of Destruction to Object of
                         Desire: The Cinematic Transformation of
                         Stevens Brown in *Les Fous de Bassan'*, *Québec
                         Studies,* 9 (1989-1990), 17-28.